In Security

Living a Confident Life

Ems Hancock

RIVER
PUBLISHING

River Publishing & Media Ltd
info@river-publishing.co.uk

ISBN 978-1-908393-56-2
Cover design by www.spiffingcovers.com

Contents

Book 1 in the

HEIRS
AND
GRACES

Series

Dedication

In memory of my deeply-loved Grandpa, George Valentine Roberts who spent much of his life as a Gideon, working tirelessly to get Bibles into hotels, prisons and schools. At the age of 90, Grandpa expressed a desire to go to University to complete a writing course.

Grandpa, you taught me that you are never too old to learn something new about the Lord. This book is for you.

Acknowledgements

To Father God, for the wonderful dream that gave me this book, its title and contents. You are so faithful!

To my wonderful husband, Jon, thank you for always encouraging me to dream big, love generously and sow deeply.

Thanks to Tim for believing in me all those years ago and for continuing to choose to champion my writing.

Thank you to each of our four amazing children – Sam, Ben, Tom and Mrs Bean – for helping me enjoy life to the full.

Thank you to my family – especially my wonderful brothers, Barnes, Dan and Jo, who have such a big place in my heart. Your sis loves you!

Thank you Daddy and Stephanie for always getting excited every time God does something awesome for us!

Thank you to my sisters-in-law, Sam, Beth and Eva. I love each of you so deeply and am excited about our future as a family x

Thank you to Anthony and Zoe and everyone at the amazing group of Ivy Churches for all your love, support and craziness!

To our darling friends Ian and Jen, for all you have done to grow my confidence, teach me who I am and speak into my life. Oh yeah, and make me cry with laughter on a regular basis! I couldn't be more grateful.

Thank you to Andy and Lucy for your togetherness in this season. It's a wonderful privilege to share daily life with you. You are beautiful people! I love your FACES!

For my Ninjas, Jo and Han, for being faithful in prayer, uber fun and freakin' awesome life companions.

Thanks to one of my total heroes, Burger. A constant servant, a brilliant husband, Dad and great friend to us. And again, ruddy hilarious! You and Han have always been so supportive of all God does in me and I love who you are.

And not forgetting our amazing Grow Group – especially our amazing MattMatt and Lulu. I love you guys!

To all my special friends in Manchester … Thank you for being you.

What Others Are Saying...

"I encourage you to read this book. Ems has a wonderful way of helping us to hold up a mirror, but instead of seeing our own reflection, she helps us to see Jesus."
Alan Charter (aimlower.com/about)
Facilitator for the Global Children's Forum and Chair of Home for Good

"I lecture on 'Confident Leadership' because the best leaders are always the most secure. You'll never fulfil the potential you were made for until you grapple with this issue and Ems will help you do so brilliantly. This book will make you laugh and think in equal measure."
Anthony Delaney, (anthonydelaney.com)
Leader of Ivy Churches and NewThing Europe

"Ems will draw you in (because she's funny) and then smack you hard with some deep wisdom that will mean you'll never be the same again! You will seriously love this book."
Andy Smith
Creative Arts Team Leader of Ivy Churches, www.ivyworship.org

"Thoughtful, honest and thought provoking, this book had an instant effect on my thought patterns and internal dialogue. It's made me want to be a better person and to let go of the junk I've been gorging on, which has left me emotionally and spiritually glum."
Gemma Hunt (gemmahunt.com)
TV presenter and Alpha Course Film Host

"The title says it all! Ems is a woman who walks out this message on a daily basis. 'Con' and 'fidence' literally means 'with' and 'faith' and Ems is one person who can deliver this great teaching in bundles! I'm really looking forward to seeing what waves this book makes in transforming people to walk out their lives in true confidence, love and grace. 10 points Ems!"

Lindz West
LZ7 & Light, www.lz7.co.uk

This book nails it ... getting to the heart of all those niggling little thoughts about ourselves that take the life out of life. The writing is warm, funny and wise, and the chapters are full of practical tips as well as deep insights. Ems has a way of saying it like it is, then saying it like it should be, and then saying it like it actually *can be*. Some books leave you longing for change ... this book has you getting up and doing something positive to transform things."

Lyndall Bywater
Freelance trainer, writer and consultant specialising in prayer
http://lyndallbywater.net

"In this book Ems shares with wisdom and vulnerable self -reflection, gently prodding us to face our own insecurities. Always writing with honesty, humility and a large dose of humour, Ems passionately points us to the only One worth putting our security in."

Ian Henderson
Founder of VISIBLE and The Naked Truth Project
http://visibleministries.com

The Bit Before The Main Bit

We only get one life – one chance to live well.

I want to live a full life with as many adventures for God as possible. I want to dare to dream, to think big and to press in to all He has for me. That doesn't mean that I need fame and fortune. Far from it. But I have realised I can't have that kind of fulfilling existence if I'm always worrying about my hair. Or my weight. Or why I can't understand algebra.

I need to create as much room as possible in my head for those wonderful, unselfish thoughts that God can drop in. I want to be ready when He says, "Go!" I want to feed the hungry with good things. I want my words to bless and heal. I want my life to count and to mean something.

I don't want to look back and wish I had had more fun, worried less about money or had more confidence. I want an adventurous life! The great news is that I have been promised one. It has been guaranteed for me.

Jesus Himself told us in His word that He came for that very purpose – so that we could have an amazing life, one lived to the max (see John 10:10).

So I don't want to blow it. I don't want to waste a day or struggle through, merely surviving. I want to live a confident life NOW, in total security.

As I have been writing this book I have been learning to practice what I am preaching. When people have made an off-the-cuff, hurtful comment, I have felt myself responding differently, from a place of confidence not insecurity. I hope reading this book allows you to do the same.

In these next few chapters we will go on a little journey together, you and I. We will discover how God's heart is always turned TOWARDS us, not against us. We will see again how precious we are and how little time there is for panic, fear and self-centredness.

There is a world out there that is desperately in need of love, hope, joy and peace. It is our job to get off that comfy sofa, get out there and make some deliveries people!

Others need what we have.

Ems Hancock

"If you have no confidence in self,
you are twice defeated in the race of life.
With confidence, you have won
even before you have started."

Marcus Tullius Cicero

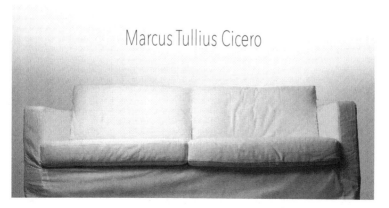

1
Insecurity Alarm

[the truth that everyone is insecure]

One of my mother's most fascinating friends was a little-known novelist and crime writer. She once asked us both to tea. As I sat in her front room, eating cake and studiously avoiding one of her large, enthusiastic dogs, I joked that I might now be a new character in one of her books.

"I wouldn't worry about that," she said jovially, in her clipped "Received Pronunciation". Closing her eyes briefly and shaking her head like many academics I have been lectured by, she delivered the immortal line,

"I don't find you nearly interesting enough to write about!"

Ouch.

I mean OUCH!

In some ways that put down was a compliment. This lady only wrote about the people in her world who baited or crossed her and she was known to be a teeny bit vicious if she counted you as a foe. But it was a put down nonetheless and one I smarted from for years to come.

I began to wonder if I was actually quite dull.

I thought about it for some time and decided, eventually, that I was not.

I still agree with myself. I am not boring. I am quite nice. I am a greatly flawed human with a huge propensity to love and learn and laugh. I do my own head in. Regularly. But no one could describe me as *dull*. I am quite fun. You can ask my friends. Or better still, my kids.

But, the fact that I spent so long considering this lady's comment did show me something about myself. Namely this: I cared too much what she and others thought about me. It showed me that I was *insecure*.

Yuck.

I hate that word.

I hate that I can be insecure. But it's true. I am insecure and so are you. So is everyone you know. And everyone I know. Some, more than others.

We all have what I call an "insecurity alarm" that a certain kind of person will set off. Perhaps it is the mum who can run up a set of curtains in an hour, or bake a flawless Victoria Sponge worthy of *Bake Off*, or run marathons, or foster 7 extra kids a year without the slightest hint of fluster.

Perhaps it's the guy who looks like George Clooney or the man who has the great clothes or whose new business wins awards, or who has a neat, shiny, size-12 wife?

Whoever it is, someone you know will both find and press your alarm. It will go off loudly and it (and they) will annoy you.

How do you deal with that?

Well, I hope this book will help.

DOWN TO THE WIRE

Years ago we were woken in the middle of the night by our own burglar alarm. It was alarming to say the least. Mainly because we didn't know we had a burglar alarm! (Well, we did, but we had never used it and assumed it was broken). We quickly ruled out the presence of an actual burglar. We also established that our burglar alarm was loud enough to wake the entire population of Poland! We were desperate. It was awful. I can still remember the sight of all of our bleary-eyed children on the stairs asking what was the matter and why the "big bell" was ringing.

Jon rang the faded number on the keypad. A tired and apathetic voice eventually answered. The man on the phone was not at all sure what we had to do.

"I am new to the alarm business," he confessed.

Brilliant.

In no apparent hurry, he finally located and thumbed through an ancient manual and told Jon that he had to "cut the wire into the box."

My husband ran to get a set of pliers.

Then the man told Jon to cut the "green" wire. Just as Jon was about to cut the green wire, the man changed his mind.

"No, Cut the brown one," he said.

"Well, which is it? The green or the brown?" Jon asked, as I stood, frantically holding as many of the kids as I could and trying to stop our collective ears bleeding.

"The brown one. It says the brown one," The sleepy man repeated.

We closed our eyes and prayed as Jon tentatively cut the brown wire. The ringing stopped. The relief was immense.

The children went back to bed. We had cut the power supply to the box and it never bothered us again.

In the same way, we need to find the root of our insecurity and cut it off at the source. Many of us try to do this, but we cut the wrong wire. We wonder why we are still insecure and why the alarm is still ringing.

In Genesis 3:1 we read,

"Now the serpent was more crafty than any of the wild animals the LORD God had made. He said to the woman, 'Did God really say, "You must not eat from any tree in the garden"?'"

Note this: The first thing the serpent does in the Bible is ask the question, "Did God really say?" This introduces Eve to an unfamiliar feeling: The feeling of *insecurity*.

Until that point she and Adam had been totally secure. They had no worries or fears. They had enough to eat. They didn't notice that they may have been slightly chilly. They were happy to gad about in the garden, unencumbered by clothing of any kind.

But now they had a new companion: DOUBT.

They doubted God. They doubted themselves. They doubted each other. They doubted the snake. They doubted that they suited fig leaves.

Insecurity is based on doubt.

It asks deep questions like, "Do I matter? Am I important? Am I loved?" It also asks shallower questions like, "Do I suit this skirt? Can I get away with this haircut? Do these glasses make me look German?"

To add to insecurity there is nearly always a large helping of what I call "comparisonitis".

"Am I prettier than her? Can I deliver a presentation better than him? Do I eat as loudly as her?"

FAKE-OVER

If I were to ask you to show me the most secure person you know, I doubt you would point firmly and squarely at yourself. Why? Because, if we are truly honest, most of us battle with deeply-rooted and shallow insecurities too, don't we? Even Madonna, the pointy-corset-endowed Queen of Pop herself, is quoted as saying:

"I think my biggest flaw is my insecurity. I'm terribly insecure. I'm plagued with insecurities 24/7."

Like Madonna, I think we are facing a kind of insecurity epidemic in our culture today. We have never had to work so hard to make it look as though everything is effortless. Our nude-look simple makeup can take us hours to apply; our salt water hair spray for that "just got out of bed" style needs a full 40-minute "fake-over" using four different appliances. We are toiling hard to make it look like we are meandering along at a chilled-out pace.

Young people are trying to fit in and stand out at the same time. They want to look normal and also quirky. They try to be part of the crowd and yet stand out from the crowd. Poor. Little. Loves.

As adults we want to be ahead of the Jones's, but also liked by the Jones's. We want to be envied by the Jones's and yet we would quite like the Jones's to put our bins back on rubbish day. In short, many of us are both confused and terrified of what people think of us and what we think of ourselves.

Even as I began to write this book I started to hear a voice in my head saying, "Who are you to think you can write about this issue?" Let's count this sentence and the rest of the book, as my reply.

Of course, our insecurities take many forms. They might seem minor to an onlooker, but they will occasionally keep us awake at night. Our flaws, our foibles and our faults can all find such inflated places in our thought–life that they appear to be grotesque, outsized exaggerations of reality. The spot on our face can reach bouncy-castle like proportions; the middle-aged spread around our girth can feel like the sagging tyre of doom in the underbelly of our imagination. Our inability to cook or count or craft becomes crazily important. Nothing is too small to miss the attention of the insecure and critical mind.

We are a sorry lot at times.

But I think I have found something that beats insecurity to a pulp. And it is for this reason that I chose to write this book. Let me explain.

One of the best moments in the animation *The Incredibles* is where Helen and Bob are arguing about Bob's clandestine superhero work. Pleading with him to focus on the needs of the family she turns to him and shouts, "This is not about YOU!"

I want you to understand something about your life. *It is not about YOU*. Hear me out. This might sound a bit weird, but I don't believe you were born for your benefit. You are not here to please yourself and you were not put on earth to make yourself happy.

I recently heard a talk by the wonderful Bill Johnson of Bethel Redding, in which he said something along these lines

– and this is not a direct quote – "Be prepared that God may want to do things *through* you and not just *for* you."

That blew me away.

Being alive for our own benefit is as crazy as a cherry tree being created to eat its own fruit. It is not the nature of things. We are here for a deeper purpose.

Put another way, a river isn't there for no reason. It is meant to sustain and nurture life, in and around itself.

The truth is that you and I are designed to do this too. We are meant for more than we can see right now. As C. S. Lewis beautifully put it in *Mere Christianity*, "If I find in myself desires which nothing in this world can satisfy, the only logical explanation is that I was made for another world."

We were made for another time and another place. We were made for Heaven. But before that, there is the business of living on earth to enjoy and conquer.

I think that in order to live well we need to understand our insecurities and hit them head on with a deft and skilled punch. We must not let them rule us, or ruin us, or reign in us.

Can I hear an "Amen"?

Thank you.

SHELF-HELP

In 2014 a staggering $549 million was spent in America on so called "self-help" books. The Internet is full to bursting with life coaches, psychologists and counsellors of every kind offering all sorts of insecurity-busting advice.

I don't want this book to find its way into that kind of pile in your life. This is not designed to be a self-help tome. It's not the sort of book that will glibly tell you to "believe in yourself more" or to "visualise your success".

Nor will I tell you anywhere to adopt a large bear-like pose before an important meeting to make yourself take up more space and imagine yourself to be bigger than you are. (I mean, think of the spectacle in the waiting room before a job interview! Awkward!) But, if you read self-help books about confidence, which I have in order to research this book, you will find such mirth-making suggestions.

I am not going to tell you to act like a big, old, angry bear. Why? Because those kinds of phrases and visualisations are not rooted in an understanding of who we really are. You are not a bear. You were never meant to be a bear.

I am learning that all of what and who I am is not found in my own success or ability at all. It is not in my dress size, my exam results, or my ability to play an instrument. It is not found in my facial features or my bank account. It is not in the recipes I cook or the places I go. It is not in the car I drive, the clothes I wear or even the **FONT** I type in.

So what is my security found in then?

My husband? My kids? My church? Or, heaven help me, my weight?

Nope.

It is found in who I belong to and in my inheritance.

ON THE TEAM

You see, my Dad is a King and He owns everything. I will inherit all of that one day. So this is who I am. The daughter of the most mighty King there has ever been or ever will be. I belong to Him. Everything He has is mine in Jesus. It's coming to me, but I have to reach out for it and believe it is there BEFORE I can see it. That is what it means to have faith. I have to trust that I belong on *His* team.

When I was at school I was miserable at sport. In fact I was miserable *about* sport. Sport of any kind made me feel as though I was officially RUBBISH. I wasn't like Lorraine Gardner who could return a serve in Tennis so low it would kiss the net and arrive at the far edge of the court just out of your reach. I wasn't like Caroline Preston who could run round a palatial park at speed with no apparent effort.

No.

I was the overweight one who always wanted a note from the Doctor to excuse me from every games lesson. I didn't belong. I looked bad in airtex and shell suits. (It was the 1980's. It was Liverpool. Forgive me. I was young.) Shell suits accentuated my flabby, unkempt body and lycra was most certainly my enemy.

Earlier this year I decided to change all that. At the age of 42 I started to lose weight. I joined a gym, got myself an amazing personal trainer, taught myself how to run and entered a 10k race. Suddenly I belonged to a new world.

Instead of envying the joggers along my road (or wanting to trip them up), I waved to them happily as I jogged past them. Suddenly I belonged. Lycra was my friend. Black Lycra anyway.

To belong in a spiritual sense means to be included, affiliated to, allied with, connected, linked, owned by, at the disposal of and safe in the arms of GOD Himself.

I believe that God wants us to feel loved, accepted and secure in Him. He doesn't want us to wait miserably in the rain by the wall as all the good players are picked. We are picked FIRST by Him. He wants us on His team. This is our inheritance. This is His desire for us. This is why we don't have to feel like the most insecure person in all of Insecureland.

SERVING SUGGESTION

Most food comes with a serving suggestion. The manufacturers provide an illustration. Even on a packet of cornflakes there will usually be a photograph. What is the photo telling us? It is saying, "We suggest that you eat these cornflakes with milk, in a bowl, using a spoon. We have taken a picture for you so that you know exactly what we mean by the terms, bowl, milk and spoon."

It couldn't be simpler. They do not suggest you put the cornflakes on a plate, or that's what the picture would show. They do not suggest that you serve them with olive oil. They know that would taste vile. The options are narrower, but they are clear about how the product will taste the best. Why? Because they are the makers.

Did you know that our lives also have a serving suggestion? The suggestion is that we *serve*. This will make us happy. The Bible is like the photograph of the food, showing us what we need in order to live well, think well and be well. The Bible shows us how to be secure. We will look into more of this later on in this book.

A wonderful verse in Isaiah 54:17 says this:

"But no weapon that is formed against you shall prosper, and every tongue that shall rise against you in judgment you shall show to be in the wrong. This [peace, righteousness, security, triumph over opposition] is the heritage of the servants of the Lord..." (Amplified Version)

Can you see how important this verse is?

It says:

1. Nothing working against us will win.
2. Every enemy will be silenced.
3. Peace, righteousness, security and triumph is our heritage.
4. We are God's servants.

As servants and children of our heavenly Dad, we have an inherited right to security. It is what God wants, intends and makes available for us.

So why is it that we struggle to *feel* secure? Why is it that our "insecurity alarms" still ring in the middle of the night? Why do we pore over magazines and berate ourselves for not looking like the airbrushed xylophone-ribbed models inside? I think it is simply because we forget who we are.

UNLIKELY HERO

One of my favourite characters in the whole of the Bible is Moses. For me, Moses is one of the most genuine heroes in all of Scripture. He is so very human. And because of this, his story is incredibly inspiring.

Moses was rescued in a miraculous way from a baby-killing maniac. He then went to live in the palace of said maniac and somehow God engineered that his own Hebrew mother was able to care for him. He lived, while all of his contemporaries died. He was saved. They were not. Surely this would have made him think? He must have known that he was special, set apart and meant for greatness. His mother must have whispered some of the miracle of his survival to him. And yet, his story is littered with self-doubt.

25

Some years later Moses sees an Egyptian beating a Hebrew and, incensed, kills him. Terrified of the repercussions of this, he runs away. He runs from his problems and wanders around in the desert for 40 years. 40 years! That is a long time at school. That is a long degree. That is a long PhD. That is a long double doctorate! Forty years of not knowing who he was or why he was alive. Maybe he had to learn a few things twice, or the hard way? At any rate, he stayed where he was all that time.

Remember that he was trained and raised to be a prince. He was not some kind of Bear Grylls. He was unlikely to have studied "desert survival training" as part of his education. There he was, not knowing which cacti he could eat and which would poison him. He probably did not know how to find food or water. He did not have a GCSE in solar-resistant, wind-proof, animal-protected, tent making. He was a guy alone in a desert. A criminal and an outcast. He had to learn the hard way.

I bet during that time the enemy came to him and jeered at him saying, "Where is the God of the Hebrews now? You can't do anything right. Look at where you are! You got it all wrong didn't you? You have failed yourself and your people. Why did your mother call you 'Drawn out?' What kind of name is that for a nomad?! You haven't been drawn out of anything at all! Let's re-name you shall we? How about 'Washed out'? That suits you better!"

We are not told, of course. I am just guessing. Guessing because I know the kind of language the enemy likes to use too well.

Sometime during this period, Moses begins to meet up

with his purpose and destiny. He meets Jethro who offers him a job. This high-flying, high-minded, high-tempered prince of Egypt with fine clothes and gold jewellery was asked to watch a few smelly animals. Talk about a come down! Moses, who had never had a job in his life and who had spent his formative years in a palace with slaves and servants to wash his clothes and feed him grapes – that guy - is now looking after sheep! Wow!

Put yourself in his sandals. He must have felt identity-less, worthless and insecure, mustn't he? He must have thought that he had been wrong to dream and hope in the God of the Hebrews. What good is Egyptology and a Phd in Sanskrit when all you have to do each day is find pasture?

So had God got it wrong?

Or had Moses himself got it wrong?

The enemy doesn't care which one of those we shout "YES!" to. He just doesn't want us to realise that our promises are on the way, or that desert seasons are meant for our good. Not at all. He wants us to whine and moan and curse God. He wants us to doubt ourselves and miss our calling.

But it is by becoming a shepherd that God can start to do business with Moses. As the story is told in the Bible, we know that Moses had an epiphany. God, the master and maker of the wonderful word "suddenly" changes his destiny and his purpose in an instant. Notice that there is no prayer prayed, no prophecy given, no speaking in tongues, no sermon preached, no course passed, no person encouraging him nearby. God appears out of nowhere, in the middle of nothing and announces that the ground Moses is standing on is HOLY ground.

Moses may well have been within his rights to argue. I mean, this was presumably ground he had stood on before, slept on before and led his sheep to before. Perhaps the sheep had even nibbled at the bush itself – the bush that was now on fire?

But now Moses was about to learn, as we have to learn too, that his destiny is IN the fire. But Moses struggles to grasp this. When he sees a bush not burning away, and audibly hears the voice of God telling Him to go somewhere (something many of us *long* for) he *still* wonders if he is the right man for the job. You can almost see him looking behind himself to check no other bearded man is standing there!

Moses was a man with an identity crisis. He wasn't Hebrew enough to be a proper Hebrew and he wasn't Egyptian enough to be an Egyptian. He was, in all honesty, a misfit.

Ever felt the same?

Ever felt that you don't fit into your family, or your church, or your neighbourhood, or your job, or your office environment, or your school? I think at times we can all feel this. But we have to recognise that being a misfit is often part of God's methodology. It's not some kind of huge cosmic mistake. It is totally intentional and designed by Him for your purpose and destiny – and for mine. God wants us to learn that our security isn't about how well we fit the moulds or about how good we have been. He wants us to be in secure IN HIM and in who He is.

Whilst he was definitely a hero, Moses was also at times, an insecure, babbling wreck of a man. This guy was a murderer with a stammer and a fear of snakes. But God saw greatness in him. In fact, God rescued him and made him a rescuer.

Nothing Moses had learnt was wasted. God was teaching him every step of the way, through every circumstance and situation. Being a shepherd helped. Being able to navigate the wilderness helped. Being a prince by background helped. Being a murderer on the run helped. Being an ordinary man who had lost his sense of duty, calling and purpose helped. God *knew* what He was doing.

If Moses had taken the Hebrews with him into the wilderness 40 years before, he would have led them into the same mess he had got himself into. He needed the credibility and experience of survival in that tough place to be able to lead those people out of it and through it.

SNAKES AND LADDERS

Isn't it wonderful that God can take the disconnected pieces of your life, the parts that make no sense, the hurts, disappointments, achievements, griefs, successes, abject failures, and turn them into something that makes sense? He specialises in this!

But we can easily forget this about God can't we? I know that I can look at the power of the Pharaohs in my life and remember all their training and count their horses. I can forget that on my team is the person who made those horses in the first place!

Fortunately, God understands this kind of insecurity. He knows where it comes from and He speaks directly to it. In Exodus 4 we see how God tackles Moses' fears and self-doubt head on. He does so with a simple stick and a not-so-simple trick. God uses something Moses already has. (I am learning that this is one of God's favourite games. It's the

"Look what I can do with what you already have" game. But Moses hadn't learnt the rules yet).

God speaks to Moses, asking him to throw his shepherd's crook on the ground. Moses does so. It turns into a snake. This is a pretty crazy party trick isn't it? God is trying to teach Moses the game.

He then asks Moses to pick the snake up by the tail. When he does so, it turns back into a stick. If that had been me, I would have been a bit scared to hold that stick, you know? But Moses is learning.

Then God tells Moses to put one of his hands into his cloak. As he pulls it out it is covered in the skin disease, leprosy.

What do the snake and the leprosy have in common? It wasn't until I was writing this actual paragraph that I suddenly realised something. According to the Talmud a snake is unclean and cannot be eaten (or is not Kosher) because it crawls along the ground. People who had leprosy were also considered to be unclean. Perhaps God was trying to show Moses that He was in charge of making him clean and acceptable (or unclean and unpalatable) to others?

God instructs Moses to put his hand back inside his cloak, and when Moses pulls it out, his hand has become normal again. Another amazing trick!

Moses had seen these two miracles and the miracle of the burning bush. He had heard the audible voice of God. He had been rescued as a baby from the madness of a sadistic king, but he still doubted.

Exodus 4:10 in the Message version reads:

"Moses raised another objection to God: 'Master, please, I don't talk well. I've never been good with words, neither

before nor after you spoke to me. I stutter and stammer.'"

He wants someone else to do this job for him! You can almost see him mentally reaching for his phone to speedial his speech therapist for an excuse note! But this assignment isn't like the PE lesson I mentioned earlier. He can't talk his way out of this. God knows him too well.

I feel so sorry for him. He needs so much reassurance doesn't he? He was tuned in to the voice of his own insecurity. He had it on constant. Insecurity speaks in a certain tone. It reminds us of the worst of ourselves and highlights the best of everyone else. It accuses and belittles us. It reminds us of our stammers not our strength.

We are so like Moses. In our way and in our situations we can forget the goodness of God. We can panic when things don't go the way we are hoping and praying for. We are quick to forget our miracles. We see God healing someone one week and doubt He can answer our prayers the next. We experience a breakthrough, but don't remember it the next time we need one.

At times we can be filled with raging insecurity that hammers us with self-doubt. We wonder how God could ever speak to us or use us or anoint us for any job at all. And then we take a big dose of self–pity and feed our doubts a little until they GROW even bigger.

But this is not what we were made for! It is not what God had in mind for Moses, or for us. Life is not meant to be a bed of roses, of course. Moses' calling was dangerous and hard. But, he was not being asked to go it alone. He was going hand in hand with a God who said, "Tell them I AM is with you."

This is what we need to speak out over our insecurities. Every single, miserable, last one of them. *God is with us.* He is for us, not against us. Each of those truths are like a safe rung on a ladder, taking us from one level of security to the next.

I AM is with us.

Insecure (adjective): uncertain or anxious about oneself, not confident (Oxford Dictionary).

Truth from this chapter:

Everyone is insecure

Life is not about me

Being secure means knowing who I belong to

Being alive and fulfilled is about serving

I am on God's team. He has picked me for a purpose.

Even if I don't fit in to other people's expectations, I fit in with God.

God can use everything that happens to me for my good.

God is with me.

2
Security Camera

[how do you see yourself?]

"Most of our great-great-grandmothers had access to compare themselves to a few hundred women in a lifetime. We can now throw ourselves up against tens of thousands..."
– Beth Moore

STATUS SYMBOL

Never before in the whole of human history have we been able to compare ourselves to so many people. Years ago, we would only have known about the inhabitants of our village or town, but now we can see what people look like on the other side of the world. And do you know what? It makes us forget who is on the other side of our street. Our telescopic vision means we can miss what is happening all around us.

We can easily find ourselves caught up in the nonsense of our celebrity culture. In the past, in order to be famous, people needed to have created something beautiful, stopped something awful or worked for something worthwhile. Now our magazines and blog sites are full of people who are famous because they are "famous". We find ourselves fascinated with total strangers having teeth whitening procedures, skin tucks and botox. Through unhelpful paparazzi photography of poor folk simply trying to get out of their houses, we eagerly monitor celebrity weight loss or gain. Nothing is private in our world of social media craziness. This is deeply unhealthy. We don't need this kind of polluted tributary coming into the river of our thinking.

Our problem is that we compare our "inside lives" to other people's "outside lives". We look at their Instagram-worthy snapshot and compare it to our inner, aching low. Envy is at a new all-time high. It comes to us every day in photos, tweets and social media statuses. This can feed our insecurities and balloon them into greater ones.

I am less than keen.

Online society has its uses, of course. It's great when you want to rally people behind a cause or show them a funny cat video. But it doesn't beat an actual cuppa with a real mate.

INTERNAL CCTV

Everywhere we go we are under surveillance. CCTV footage witnesses the most banal and mundane of our daily activities - from buying a pair of socks to standing in line at the Post Office. Our actions are all being caught on some tediously inexorable film.

Can you imagine what it would be like though if there was an *internal* CCTV that showed what people – what you and I – were actually thinking?

I think our internal CCTV thoughtlife is a bit scary. Why? Because it is:

- dependent (on how we feel)
- changeable
- innacurate
- biased
- surface
- based on comparison

How others see us is also all of these things because it depends on circumstances or on what we have done or said. Our views about ourselves are based on imperfect motives and imbalanced opinion.

We can't help it! We are only human! How we see ourselves and others depends on what we are looking at.

There was once a professor who asked his students to look at a screen and tell him what they could see.

Every eye in the room intently studied the display. There was nothing on the screen except for a small black dot.

Every hand shot up and voice after voice said, "I can see a small black mark."

"You are all right," he said. "But I can also see a lot of white space. The black dot is very small in comparison to all the white."

The problem with our lives is that we look at the problems in them. We make that the thing we worry about, talk and obsess about. Even if life is going well, we seem to be able to find the one "black spot" and focus on that. We tune in to the imperfections, don't we?

TRASH TALK BULLYING

We do this with ourselves too. The truth is that many of us are terrible bullies – not out loud to other people, but inside to ourselves. We call ourselves every name under the sun! We shout at ourselves internally that we are,

UGLY

STUPID

FAT

LAZY

POINTLESS

USELESS

FORGETFUL

DISORGANISED

UNKIND

BAD

POOR (PARENTS, SIBLINGS, FRIENDS)

INADEQUATE

NOT AS GOOD AS...

IDIOTS

Just think for a minute and re-read that list. When did you last call yourself one of those names? Be honest!

We would be so shocked if anyone else said those things to us and, of course, would never DREAM of saying them to our closest friends. But we wander through life content to say these dreadful things over and over again *to ourselves!* We speak to ourselves in a way we were not designed to be spoken to. Some of us speak the language of lies – the worship language of hell – over our hearts on a daily basis. This is incredibly dangerous for the soul. It makes us feel miserable, and as though we have failed before we have even started the day and properly opened our eyes.

It hurts God when we bruise ourselves in this way. He knows it is a form of self-harm that is addictively powerful. It makes us believe we are less than we are. It is also fills our minds with negativity, trash talk and nay-saying. It reminds us of the problems and the pain. It does not look for words of power, purpose or praise.

FAKE HUMILITY

I remember challenging someone on her self-talk and she told me she was trying to "keep herself humble". I suppose bad-mouthing yourself can feel to some like a kind of humility. But of course it is not. To deprecate, disparage and downgrade yourself is not humility, but a form of *self-humiliation*. And there is a big difference.

Humility tells the truth about what we are and what we are not. Humiliation tells lies about what we are and what we are not. They are opposite spirits. True humility is beautiful. Humiliation never can be.

What we say about and to ourselves is tremendously important. I get so sad when I hear people putting themselves down. It is an ugly trait from an ugly source.

WATCH YOUR MOUTH!

I once sat one of my friends down and told her straight that I had noticed how often she put herself down. She did it in a jokey way, but they were negative comments all the same. She thanked me for pointing out this habit. She knew she did it, but didn't see it as a problem. After I told her how uncomfortable it made me, she sat up and took notice. You see, every time she made those self-rejecting statements she undermined what I thought of her. It actually began to make ME feel rejected. I had chosen her to love and invest in her and share life with her. But her words were constantly against herself – as if I was making a bad choice of friend. We had a chat and a hug and a pray. She could see what I meant. She has been amazing in her self-talk ever since. I now think she has a much better attitude about herself and certainly operates using healthier language.

I'm not saying we can't be honest about ourselves – sometimes we need to be vulnerable, and painfully so. But I am talking about the constant bullying, biting, criticism that so often dances fiendishly in the mouths and minds of the insecure.

MOOD LIGHTING

It is easy for us to talk negatively about our lives.

All we have to do is take our eyes off Jesus and we can be sucked into a vacuum of despair. Many of us need help to change the "mood lighting" of our day.

Did you know that the first four minutes of the morning can often set up the whole day for you? Either as an epic, adventurous fun ride of joy, or as a miserable "nobody loves me" Eeyore-type downer. It's true.

What we allow ourselves to think, say and do in those early hazy, sleepy moments is more key than we realise. If we wake up with fear about an important meeting or a work deadline or something we forgot to do, that could colour the whole day grey. (Or as fashion designers now rejoice in calling it, Battleship, Mouse-back or understated "Greige"!)

Either way, grey is not a great colour for a mood. But the good news is, you can start your day in a different way, with different thoughts and different feelings.

The Bible helps us here. In Lamentations 3:1 we read how Jeremiah speaks about himself with classic negative self-talk. He says, *"I am the man who has seen affliction..."* (v1).

That is not a great beginning. To say, "I am miserable and I have had great troubles," isn't going to start his week off well. In fact, it's even going to make his dog want to leave home! He carries on, talking of God saying,

"He has driven me away and made me walk
in darkness rather than light;
indeed, he has turned his hand against me
again and again, all day long.
He has made my skin and my flesh grow old
and has broken my bones.
He has besieged me and surrounded me
with bitterness and hardship." (v2-5)

He is not what we would call a bundle of joy is he? Can you see the downward spiral that starts here? He is reminding himself of all his troubles. He is rehashing and rehearsing and replaying them. Like an actor with a script to learn, he says negative things about himself over and over again. His words become an unhealthy list of his woes.

We can be like Jeremiah can't we? When our problems multiply or life seems unfair or cruel, our self-talk will often deteriorate too. Like Jeremiah, we can blame God for our problems. We can replay everything in an almighty list of hideousness, stuck on repeat. God gets it in the neck for Jeremiah's physical symptoms, his emotional issues and his feeling of being trapped and imprisoned. We do this to God too, don't we?

"God! You promised me that this would be a season of

growth, but I feel like there is nothing happening!"

"God you said that you would do me good and that you have good plans for my life. Why did you let this (insert bad thing) happen?"

I'm not saying we should not be real with God. Far from it. But I *am* saying we should not find every fear in our BIG BOOK OF FEARS and read it out loud three times a day.

Because what happens when we do this is that our fears grow and our faith depletes. Simply said, our problems get bigger. Our imaginations *magnify the mess.*

Jeremiah made a choice. He chose to speak out his fears. He spoke of God's apparent failure to answer his prayers, and the feeling he had that he'd been singled out by others and made a laughing stock. He sounds as though he is utterly dejected and depressed. That kind of self-talk intensifies despair, it breeds downward thinking and makes room and space for negativity.

If you can be like Jeremiah in this way, read on. There is hope!

The turning point comes when Jeremiah begins to change his manner of speaking. He decides to *remember* God's truth and His promises saying,

"This I recall to my mind, therefore I have hope. Because of the Lord's great love we are not consumed ... His compassions never fail. They are new every morning; great is Your faithfulness." (v22-23)

It is very simple and very obvious to say this, but when we change our minds, we also change our moods. Our thinking has to change before our behaviour will come into line. It won't happen immediately, but if your words change for the better you can start to set the course of your mind in a totally different direction.

When we deliberately refocus our thinking, especially at a time when we are struggling to do so, something like a light switch turns on. Why? Because suddenly we are thinking in line with the promises of God. We are agreeing with truth and aligning ourselves with ancient declarations and promises made about us in the very courts of Heaven. We are standing on ground that has been fought over and won at the cross. We are agreeing with the Boss!

It is important for us to realise that Jeremiah's situation did not change. His viewpoint did. What he allowed himself to think affected what he found himself saying, which in turn affected his thoughts. It was a faith circle.

We can change the tide of opinion over ourselves simply by speaking out the verses of truth God has already given us. When Jeremiah finally realises this, he starts to say words like:

"The Lord is good to those whose hope is in him, to the one who seeks him" (v24)

This is the total opposite of how he began! He has turned himself around by changing his self-talk.

Do you need to do the same today?

MENTORING AS A LIFESTYLE

At university I had a wonderfully precious weekly meeting with a sweet lady who became my mentor. Every Monday during term time we met to talk through one of the gospels. We chatted about what Jesus taught and how that relates to us now. It was the first time I was truly intentional about my own spiritual development. I learnt that it was absolutely vital for me to sit under the authority and teaching of others who were wiser and older than me. I also realised how much I had to learn about the Bible. This journey began an awakening in me. For the next 16 years or so I had a series of different mentors. Some were just short term but others lasted years. They were hugely varied people from diverse backgrounds, but this was wonderfully helpful to me. I met up with everyone from a Benedictine Monk to an ex-TV presenter. God certainly gave me a rich group of people to learn from!

These gracious, kind people who invested in me and sowed their lives into mine showed me more of who Jesus was and of who I was in *Him*. I think my self- esteem would be in a mess without their advice, prayers and wisdom. They helped me to think differently and stop being such a bully to myself.

In turn, I have been a mentor for a number of years now. I am a big fan of meeting up with someone who wants to invest in their own inner person. I love it when God brings me someone who He is readying for what He has next. I enjoy sitting with people, listening to their fears and their triumphs and helping them assess what God is teaching them and preparing them for.

If you have never had a mentor, can I ask you to think about it? Ask God to give you someone you can meet with regularly to ask you those challenging questions and to remind you of who you are. Or perhaps you are an older, more experienced Christian? If so, are you taking anyone under your wing right now? Is there anyone you could sow your life into and help to not make the same mistakes you have?

Having someone who believes in you and wants you to succeed is one of the most powerful hidden strengths of successful and secure people. Did you realise that someone else's security could, in part, depend on your time? It could depend on your skills, or advice, or prayers.

One of the most common things I am reminded of when I am mentored or when I am mentoring others is that *I am ME and I can't be anyone else*. I can't waste time wanting or envying anyone else's life or calling. Each of us is on earth with a specific skill set. We can learn new skills, of course, but our heart and core remain the same. What we tend to do though is look at other people's skills and envy theirs.

SEW WHAT?

Let me give you an example. I have always wanted to be able to sew. A number of years ago I bought myself a simple sewing book. Excitedly, I went through it to find my first project, but my heart sank. Even the simplest little design in the book required the use of the dreaded sewing machine.

The last time I used a sewing machine was when I was 12 years old. I accidentally sewed all 4 sides of a duvet cover together. It took me 7 weeks to unpick what I had done in my first lesson. My teacher eventually had to cut it and make it into a small tablecloth. Herself. In no uncertain terms she told me to "give up" and do something else. Sewing and I parted company and we have never been friends since.

Now, some of my best pals are fabulous sewers. I used to envy their ability to make a dress or, lets face it, even a pencil case. But now I have realised something simple and lovely. God gave them their gifts to bless me. He gave me my gifts to bless them.

They can't bake like me, or write a silly story like me. I

can't make cushions like them. So we swap life skills. We share. Together we are an awesome combination! I get so much pleasure out of making something for them and they love being able to bless me. It's a "WIN WIN" people!

Now I celebrate the fact that I can't sew, do my own self-assessment tax form, build websites or understand rudimentary music theory. I have people in my life who do that for me.

There is a wonderful exchange when we understand the bartering nature of skill-sets. I can look after your child whilst you hem my dress. You can take a photo of me whilst I make you the "mother of all cakes". Sharing is caring. It's all good.

PRACTICALLY PERFECT

When my daughter was little she loved watching Mary Poppins on DVD. I grew used to her suddenly breaking into one of the songs in the bath or as she was having her tea.

One of my favourite scenes in the film is where Mary delves into her carpet-bag to find her tape measure. Measuring the children to see what they are like she finds that Jane is "rather inclined to giggle" and "doesn't put things away". (Uncannily like myself). But when she measures herself she sees the tape measure say,

"Mary Poppins - practically perfect in every way."

I love that kind of audacious confidence! Of course, no one is perfect, but we were all made by a perfect God, who has perfect plans for us. We need to give ourselves a bit more credit.

The way we see ourselves can sometimes be very messed up. We can focus too much on the outward appearance and not on who we really are.

How do you measure yourself against others? Do you look at your jeans size or income? Our society is preoccupied with what we and others look like. I signed a petition the other day on Change.org. It was started by a 23 year-old model, Rosie Nelson, who wears a clothes size 8 to 10. She walked into one of the UK's biggest model agencies and they told her that she ticked all the boxes except one: she needed to lose more weight. So she did. Four months later she lost nearly a stone – around 2 inches off her hips. When she returned to the same agency they told her to lose more weight, they wanted her "down to the bone".

I'm glad she chose to tell people about this and try to get the tide of public opinion to turn. The truth is that beauty is nothing to do with weight. Some of the most stunning people in history weren't thin.

For me beauty is about confidence. Not brashness and arrogance, but an awareness of your place in the world, of who you are and who you belong to. When I was younger I remember someone preaching on Proverbs 31:30, *"Charm is deceptive and beauty is fleeting but a woman who fears the Lord is to be praised."*

This verse is so hard hitting. Charm is indeed deceptive. We can use charm in life to get what we want and need. I've done that and I bet you have too. You flash a winning smile to the hotelier before asking him to print a quick document. You need your mum to sew on a button, but you start by telling her the meal she just made you was amazing.

Charm can be a liar.

Beauty is fleeting too. Some of us can be stunners in our

youth but lose that quality as we age. God is not impressed by our outward appearance. He looks at the heart (1 Samuel 16:7). But maturity and security in Him is really something to be praised. Security is praiseworthy and excellent and something we should aspire to. The Bible tells us that fearing the Lord is the beginning of wisdom (Proverbs 9:10). Those who are wise are not those who battle with insecurity.

It seems to me to be very key for us to lose the craziness of insecurity as fast as we can. It is a waste of our time and our thoughts and what's more it is false advertising. It makes it seem as though life is about US. When of course it is not.

It is about others. And Jesus.

"Whoever fears the Lord has a secure fortress, and for their children it will be a refuge." (Proverbs 14:26)

Truth from this chapter:
We shouldn't compare ourselves to celebrities or strangers
We shouldn't waste time thinking about what we can't change
We shouldn't rely on our feelings to tell us accurately what we are like
We should not bully ourselves with our words
We should guard the first minutes of the day
We should watch our self-talk.
We should look at mentoring or being mentored
We should enjoy our gifts and the gifts of others
We should remember that beauty is about who we are

3
Security Alert

[things that feed our insecurities]

"I have set the Lord always before me; because he is at my right hand, I shall not be shaken." (Psalm 16:8 ESV)

UNDERGROUND TALENT

Recently as an experiment, Joshua Bell, arguably one of the world's most accomplished violinists, busked on Washington's metro system. He, and the Washington Post, wanted to see what the reaction would be to his playing from ordinary people at an ordinary moment in their day. Bearing in mind his gifting and his sell-out gigs everywhere he goes, this was an interesting premise.

So, unsuspecting commuters were treated to a virtuoso performance from a guy in a baseball cap and unassuming T-shirt. Ending his 43-minute set with an amazing rendition of Bach's D-minor Chaconne this was no ordinary busker, but people seemed not to notice his talent.

You might have imagined a crowd would develop, stop and be wowed by his playing. Perhaps Bell himself hoped that he would make the whole station come to a standstill, causing spontaneous applause as he came to an end.

However, this was not the case. Out of 1097 people who passed him (the Washington Post counted every one of them), a grand total of 7 people stopped to listen for more than a minute to him. He earned only $32 and a few cents. Not enough to get a ticket to one of his own gigs.

So what can we learn from this?

Is Bell still talented, although no one noticed? YES, of course! The beauty of his playing is not in question. It is just that so many of us are too busy to stop and notice the beauty right in front of our faces.

We are so fickle. We expect things to be showcased, dressed up and parcelled in such a way that we are "helped" to see them. The Mona Lisa is not in a grubby McDonalds in Slough. Prize portraits are given expensive gilt frames and shown in white-walled hushed spaces. Talent, beauty, fashion, perfume and music is packaged, thrown at us, critiqued and discussed.

The exercise – really a stunt, which Bell conceived over a cup of coffee with a Post journalist – actually proves the power of context.

We all perceive things within their context. We cannot easily do otherwise. We look at our lives for what they appear to be *in the now*. But we are not always right to do so.

God may be hiding something in us, or from us, that is hard to see, especially if we are too busy to stop and value it. Joshua Bell could have seen this experiment as a reason to throw in the towel and stop playing altogether. Fortunately, he did not. He knew what his talent was, even if others didn't recognise it. He was secure in who he was.

Each of us will have times in our lives when our insecurities get the better of us. We may have bad days, months or even years. We may try something out and admit it was a disaster. Or we may experience a level of success, but not what we were hoping for.

But what is it that grows our insecurity and shakes our security levels? It is true that we live in a highly negative society. Bad news is good news for newspapers and blog sites but not great for our souls. Just waking up and reading a summary of what has happened around the world can make us feel low. Now that we have the ability to know the news whenever we are ready to hear it, we are exposed to crime, violence and bombarded by global crises 24/7.

Many circumstances of life can throw us off and make us reel around, uncertain of ourselves for a while. Perhaps, but not exclusively we may be suffering from:

- The perhaps unmerited or fast success/popularity of others
- Disappointment and discouragement
- Lack of honour
- Abuse
- Pride/ego
- Wrong opinion of self
- Wrong opinion of God
- Fear
- Depression or other mental illness
- Health worries
- Grief or loss

I don't know if you are struggling in one or more of these

areas. From my own experience I know how hard some of them can be. I am going to take each of these things in turn and look at them briefly in the light of what the word of God says. So lets start with a painful one...

THE SUCCESS OF OTHERS

How do you cope when others around you gain favour, win, succeed or get their prayers answered? Do you pat their back with gritted teeth and a fake smile or are you able to be genuinely happy for them?

When I got my first book deal one of my besties sent me this wonderful short email which simply said:

"THIS FLOODS MY HEART WITH JOY! XXX"

There was no rivalry in those words. She was crying happily for me. She had sat and prayed with me for my breakthrough to the point where she was experiencing it WITH me. God loves it when we are genuinely able to rejoice with those who rejoice. But there are times when this kind of rejoicing is painful, difficult or even feels impossible aren't there?

Jon and I had been married for a couple of months before we started talking about having children. I was so excited about the thought of being a mum and felt so ready to embrace that whole season in my life. But no babies came.

We prayed and hoped and prayed some more. It was hard at this time to witness other friends of ours getting pregnant quickly and easily, whilst I would cry every time my monthly cycle appeared. It was difficult for me to rejoice with my friends because I felt like I was in a season of mourning.

There are many reasons why we can find ourselves in a place where we feel "less than." Perhaps we feel less worthy, less attractive, less amusing, less talented, less valued, less popular, less intelligent, less wealthy, less cared for or even less loved than those around us.

We see their success in an interesting and definitive way. What I am about to say is massively HUGE for us to grasp. When God showed me this recently it stopped me in my tracks. *We can sometimes see other people's success as our apparent failure.*

Wow! It's true. I can sometimes see things in that way and I think you can too, can't you? We can't help seeing other people's success through the lens of our own apparent lack. Do you see what that means? It means that their joy reminds us of our misery. It compounds our situation and can make us feel hopeless. The Bible is so wonderful at times like this. Its comforting words are so real. In the Good News Bible Psalm 34:18 says:

"The Lord is near to those who are discouraged; he saves those who have lost all hope."

Have you lost all hope recently? Is there something in your life that makes you feel as though you are powerless and desperate? If so, my heart goes out to you right now ... But I want you to look at what this verse says. It states that God is NEAR to you in your discouragement. He is not waiting until you feel better to come to your aid, like some fair-weather friend. He doesn't need you to dry your tears and pretend you are OK. He wants you to know that He is next to you, in this moment, right now.

I hope that even in the bleakness of how you are feeling, God's hope begins to whisper to your heart. He will save you from this experience in His way and in His time. Will you choose to keep trusting and telling yourself that truth?

LACK OF HONOUR

I once spent some time in a team setting where everyone else was male, learned and older. These people had more letters after their names than I had in my whole address! I regularly felt out of my depth and as though I had nothing to offer. It was a testing time for me. My opinion was rarely given or asked for. I wasn't confident to say very much because I felt a lack of honour for me in the room. At the end of each meeting I would run to the loo and quietly sob.

Lack of honour takes many ugly forms. It belittles, bullies and betrays us. It can manifest itself in manipulation or control issues. We can be unsure of the cause of the angst in the air but feel as though the atmosphere is fraught and tight for some reason. It can make us feel afraid to be ourselves.

I wish I could go back into that team, now that I am much more confident of who I am and what I carry. But I let those men's opinion of themselves and me matter far too much and make me feel small.

In Romans 12:10 the apostle Paul exhorts us to *"be devoted to one another in brotherly love."* He goes on to say, *"Honour one another **above** yourselves"* (my emphasis). This kind of honour is counter-cultural isn't it? It goes against our natural instincts, which are to care for and value ourselves FIRST.

I was once in a small prayer meeting after a service. One of the guys started thanking God passionately for the other people in the meeting. He was praising God for their gifts and abilities and really loving and honouring them with his words. But I sat there thinking, "Why isn't he including me? Didn't

I do a good job today?" Instead of being able to agree with his prayer I was filled with insecurity and started to question my own talents. God really pulled me up on it afterwards and made me examine my heart. He told me that I needed to be a celebrator of others and get on board when others were being praised. I have never forgotten that lesson.

I don't know what has happened in your life that has made you feel a lack of honour? Perhaps someone has belittled or despised you in public, or maybe someone has lied about you or spoken ill of you or left you out of an important decision. Let me encourage you today to give that person to God and ask Him to allow the power of His beautiful forgiveness to rise up in you for that person.

Being someone who honours others is so important. As much as possible I try to be an encourager. Sometimes I will just ask God a simple question: "Who needs a word of love and blessing today?" And then I will wait. Often a friend will come into my heart. Sometimes a verse of Scripture will appear in my mind or perhaps a picture for them too. If it feels right, I will then send that to my friend.

I can't tell you how much joy God has brought to me through this habit of honouring and preferring others. It is also true that honour begets honour. It is wonderfully catching.

So, who could you honour and celebrate today?

ABUSE

Maybe you have been in a situation that got out of hand and someone damaged you with their actions or words. Maybe you are still trying to work out how you feel about that and your self-esteem has taken a real knock. I know from my own life that it can be hard to feel whole when someone has succeeded in breaking you.

For years I hoped that the people who hurt me would somehow make it right; that they would come to me with tears of repentance and help me to move on. But life isn't always like that is it? We can't wait for people to be sorry before we decide to get free. Our time on earth is too short for that. If you have been static in your journey with this and not seen any kind of breakthrough, let me ask you to look to Jesus who will grant you peace, even in the midst of your pain. Only God can heal the wounds left by verbal, physical or sexual abuse and the sooner we realise that, the more time we will have to let Him begin.

Psalm 147:3 says *"He heals the broken hearted and binds up their wounds."* What a verse that has been for me! If you could have met me years ago and seen how badly I was broken and damaged, you would see how well God has treated me and how wonderfully I have been restored.

Let God love you today. Give Him the fresh rawness or the old wound of your hurt and allow Him to carry the full weight of that. It is what He longs to do.

PRIDE/EGO

There is obviously a big difference between the kind of pride that God detests and the kind that we might feel about a job done well. God *wants* us to feel good about the work we do. This mimics Him. Remember that after He had created the heavens and the earth He looked around and remarked that, *"it was good"* (see Genesis 1:31). He was proud of Himself! He knew He had nailed it! He wants us to be like this too.

But of course, there is the other kind of self-righteous, self-referential pride. This is a barrier to seeking God and it gets in the way of us being truly happy. (It can also make us pretty hard to like and get on with).

None of us like to be wrong. We don't enjoy others lauding it over us and coming out on top. We can struggle when other people are better than us at something can't we?

Occasionally, our insecurity in one area can go so far that it can appear as arrogance or pride to others. We can show off about something that we CAN do to make up for something we can't. It's pretty horrible when we spot this in others and even worse when we see it in ourselves.

All my life I have found Maths challenging. At times, I even struggle to read phone numbers or write them correctly in a sequence. I have to check things a lot. My brain does not seem to hold information about numeracy at all well. As a child I was regularly anxious about this, especially as I was at a school full of deeply intelligent children. Because of this I used to be very sensitive around people who were really brainy in this way. I would try to find a skill they didn't have in order to make myself feel better. What a classic insecure reaction!

After my Mum and Gran died, together with our solicitor, I had to sort out their wills and be in charge of dealing with all the finances for the family. For someone with my lack of skill in this area this was truly terrifying. But God was wanting to teach me not to be afraid of numbers and to learn that I could understand the basics I needed, for myself and others.

As I have grown older I have learnt how to compensate for my issues with Maths and can now employ some simple methods to help myself. I use an App that helps me keep on top of my money and I am good at budgeting and not wasting our resources. I will never be an ace mathematician and I am OK with that. As I said earlier in the book, I know plenty of people who have different gifts to me. I employ a trustworthy accountant and I am good at asking for help. I've learnt that when people talk about Maths stuff, I don't need to sing loudly in their face or produce a prize-winning cake to compensate for my lack of gifting. I leave the algebra to them, smile and nod and go and put the kettle on.

I was brought up in the Church of England. One of the phrases I loved saying in the liturgy was, "All things come from You and of Your own do we give you" (taken from 1 Chronicles 29:14). In other words, nothing I have is mine. No talent, no gift, no ability, no financial blessing, no relationship, no possession, no idea. Nothing belongs to ME, so I can't take any credit for it. True humility realises that God is responsible for every blessing we have.

Is there an area of your life where you struggle and feel insecure? Or have you been arrogant with someone recently about one of your talents? Have you congratulated yourself on how clever you've been and forgotten to thank the God who inspired you in the first place?

Perhaps you could spend some time giving that to God now. Ask Him to show you ways of coping with your weaknesses and honouring Him with your strengths. He really cares about how we treat ourselves and others and He is so creative when it comes to solutions.

WRONG OPINION OF SELF

Maybe you have been brought up haphazardly or badly

and have a poor opinion of who you are. Perhaps you can't accept your facial features or your body type or you battle with something about your personality. Often it is the opinion of others that has damaged how we feel about ourselves. Or perhaps your abilities have been called into question by others? It is true that negative words carry more weight than positive ones. We can find it easier to recall the one negative thing that was said, than many positive things, can't we?

We can also confuse failure in a given situation with failure in life. Recently I was at a worship team meeting at church and our leader said, "Failure is an event, not a person." That really hit me. YOU are not a failure, even if you have experienced failure. It can be hard to separate the two, but we really must.

However you are feeling and whatever you have gone through there are some things about other people's opinions that I think it's helpful to remember:

Opinions matter
Opinions flatter
Opinions shatter

a) Opinions matter

Opinions, what people think and how they feel, do matter. We are built to care about what people around us feel about the way we act, dress, address personal hygiene issues or speak. Living in community means we can't be immune to the hashtag of thought out there. But we should not let it cloud our judgment. High-speed social networking means that everyone else can know an opinion on a hat or a meal they have eaten the second after they have formed that thought in their minds. More importantly, people use many social media sites now for bullying tactics and trolling purposes. We need to be careful that their opinion does not MAKE or break us.

Think about whose good opinion you currently prize. Do you think that person's opinion of you is in line with God's? If so, thank Him for their wisdom and their role in your life. Ask Him to protect that person and their relationship to you.

Think about those whose opinion has hurt you. Choose to break yourself off from that by forgiving them and ask God to continue to heal you and show you who you are.

b) Opinions flatter

There are many people out there paid to schmooze. Their job is to smoothe the way for a new person, product or programme. Their words drip with engaging phrases that can make us want or feel we need what they think we should want or need.

There may be someone in your life who has not praised you in a genuine way. Perhaps they have said something nice to you because they *wanted* something from you.

It's wonderful to remember that God never says lovely things to us because He needs something from us. He will never change his opinion of you to flatter you. He will always speak the truth.

c) Opinions shatter

I have met a number of people who are capable of being so cutting about a person or a product or an image, that it has tainted, changed and shattered other people's opinions. There have been some people in my life who have set themselves up against me, spoken negatively to or about me and refused to bless me.

I have had to learn the hard way that I will only listen to a few trusted people about my life. I take in what everyone says about me, or to me ... but I will not act on all I hear. I have my own opinion about whose opinions count for me.

Whose opinion matters to you?

My Mum was a very attractive lady but she always struggled with what she looked like – especially as she got older. She once confided in me, sadly, that her mother had never told her she was beautiful. And so, because that opinion had been withheld, she couldn't always hear it when others said she was.

I thought about that for some time and wondered why my Gran did not speak out that much-needed truth. As I looked back at old photographs of my Grandmother I saw how she hardly ever smiled. She had what she called "unfortunate teeth". Perhaps my Great Grandmother had never told her she was pretty? I don't know the reason, but I do know that what we believe about ourselves affects what we are able to genuinely say to others.

For this reason you will often hear me saying to little girls (and bigger girls) of my acquaintance, "Did you wake up even more beautiful today?" The smaller ones laugh and say, "Yes I did!" The slightly more senior ones are more bashful as they smile and shrug. The older ones can look uncomfortable and even surprised. But I keep saying it. I just want everyone to know how God sees them.

Just like my mother's opinion of herself was coloured by my Grandma, there will be people in our lives whose good opinion or praise we will long for and perhaps never receive.

One word from that person would mean more than a hundred words from another. So what if it is rare or never spoken out? Or what if negative things have been said instead?

Words can be so painful can't they? They can go to the root of who we are and throw poison over us, inhabiting our growth and stunting our emotional well-being. A lack of kind, truthful comforting words can do the same. One elderly lady once came to me after an event I was speaking at. She told me with floods of tears that her father had never told her he loved her. She had lived with the pain of those unsaid words for 80 years.

I don't know what your Mum said, or didn't say, or what your Dad did or didn't do. But I know what your Heavenly Father says about you. He couldn't be more smitten with you right now! He loves who you are and what you are. He loves how you have tried to trust Him even on dark days. He holds His hands out to you now and says, "Let me love you! Let me provide all you need."

Do you know this beautiful verse in the Bible? It's from Zephaniah 3:17 and it says this about you:

"The Lord your God is with you,
the Mighty Warrior who saves.
He will take great delight in you;
in his love he will no longer rebuke you,
but will rejoice over you with singing."

Do you know He is with you? Do you know that He can save you? Do you know He takes great delight in you and that He sings over you? You don't need to worry what anyone else thinks of you when you remember this mighty and healing truth.

I am learning (still) that what God says about me and to me is FAR more important than what others say. He sees deeper than the latest jeans, or the sunglasses, or the hem length of your skirt. He knows what battles we face and what storms rage in our hearts and He loves us in it. So what should our response be? The Psalm I started this chapter with helps us here:

"I have set the Lord always before me; because he is at my right hand, I shall not be shaken." (Psalm 16:8)

It is important to ask God what He thinks about us. This is the way to stay rooted and secure. His opinion of us is what truly matters.

WRONG OPINION OF GOD

A Jewish boy once came home from school and told his mother he had a part in the class play. She asked what he was going to be. The boy replied, "I am playing the part of the Jewish husband." The mother scowled and said, "Go back and tell the teacher you want a speaking part!"

This joke is based on a cliché, but I have known some amazing Jewish women who have been the most tenacious characters. They know who they belong to. You don't mess with a Jewish lady because they know they aren't alone.

Every Jew understands that God is a speaking God. He has a speaking part in their lives. As Christians we need to remember this too. God longs to speak to us, but some of us don't take the time to listen. We feel desperately insecure about what He might think or feel about us, but we don't go to His word, or pray, or seek His face. We just let the worry wind us up and keep us away from Him.

And of course this is exactly what Satan loves. He absolutely thrives on us seeing God wrongly as someone who can't forgive us, love us or accept us.

If you have found it hard to believe that God is FOR you, that He has the best for you and longs for you to be fulfilled and happy, please speak to Him about it. Tell Him what you are worrying about and ask Him to direct you to some answers in His word. If you don't know where to start, think of one phrase that bothers you and search using Bible Gateway or another online search tool for what the Bible says about how you are feeling. God has used this simple method in my life many times to bless and encourage me.

FEAR

What are you scared of? I mean really frightened of?

For some time now I have, somewhat irrationally, carried around a secret dread of having to deliver a baby in a taxi. Fortunately for me, some years back, one of my brothers furnished me with a copy of the "Worst case scenario survival handbook". It's been invaluable. Now, I know that I must never enter a taxi, or indeed any vehicle with a heavily pregnant woman, without a supply of clean towels and a serviceable shoelace.

What would your worst-case scenario be? Fending off a shark, jumping from a moving car, disabling a bomb or escaping from killer bees?

There are many types of fear we deal with but they can be broadly categorized into two: "Fear of Man" and "Fear of God."

a) Fear of man

What does the "fear of man" look like? Fear like this controls us. It means that we are afraid of what others think, feel, say, or do and this consumes us. Some people might call it "people pleasing" but it is actually "people-fearing" in disguise. And when we fear anyone or anything other than God, then that will become our temporary God. And what do we always do with our Gods? We serve them.

Fear of man makes us despairing. It causes us to look at the negatives. We talk about the bad things. We think about the bad things. We act upon the bad things and this makes everything feel ... well, bad. Everything we do is driven by fear. We don't want to look silly, so we do "x". We don't want to fail so we do "y". The enemy's role in our life is to speak despair to our dreams and say, "You won't get that new thing you are hoping for; you won't make anything of yourself; you'll never get through that problem in your marriage; you won't complete that project; you won't have children; you won't get out of debt; your kids will end up worse off than you; you won't have enough...." There is never any love or hope or joy in what the enemy says. An acrostic for this type of fear might be:

False

Evidence

Appearing

Real

It is fake, but it looks so darn plausible. So, let me ask you: what are you controlled by? What do you feel despairing about? What do you sense isolates you from others or from God?

I want to tell you something amazing today. I want to give

you a new definition of fear. *FEAR equals worship.* Did you get that? This will really help you if you struggle with fear. Why do I say that fear is a form of worship? Because what you fear lords it over you. It has mastery over you. You may never have thought about it like that, but it is true.

All of us from time to time will meet fears like this. But how do we respond? Remember that fear needs an environment to grow in. You can choose to feed your fears, worship them even, or you can starve them before they weaken you.

What choice will you make today?

b) Fear of God

On the other hand the "Fear of God" makes us strong and keeps us strong! An acrostic for this type of "fear" could be:

FACE

EVERYTHING

AND

RISE

Loving and worshipping God like this brings us fulfillment, life, joy, peace and hope. But it isn't always easy is it? We will still go through times of fear, we just won't do it alone.

God once said something wonderful to me that I found so moving and helpful about this. He said,

"Ems I will not remove you from the place of fear, but I will remove you from the FACE of fear."

In other words, He will turn my head to focus on Him instead. Psalm 23 says He feeds us in the midst of our enemies. He lays a banquet table for us there. Not only providing for our needs but lavishing us with His generosity. I love the fact that God chooses to do this for us. He understands the depths of our fears and stands with us in the very midst of them.

One night a mother told her little girl to go outside and get her the brush on the porch. "I don't want to go out there Mummy," said the girl. "I'm scared of the dark."

The mother smiled reassuringly. "You don't have to be, Jesus is out there. He'll look after you and protect you." The little girl looked at her mother and asked, "Are you sure He's out there?"

"Yes, I'm sure. He is everywhere, and He is always ready to help you when you need Him," she replied.

The little girl thought about this for a minute and then went to the back door and cracked it open a little. Peering out into the darkness, she called, "Jesus? Can you please hand me Mum's brush?"

God loves us to go to Him when we are afraid. But He won't do everything for us. We have to face our fears and go out into the dark. We have to choose to worship Him even when we are afraid. He loves to be our hiding place.

DEPRESSION OR OTHER MENTAL ILLNESS

I don't know what you are facing right now that is keeping you in a place of insecurity. Perhaps it is depression or another kind of mental illness that is pulling you back and causing you to struggle to feel loved and whole.

One of the hardest things about battling with the mind is how tiring it is. If this is how you are feeling today, the Bible speaks these comforting, hope-filled words to your heart right now:

Isaiah 40:31 says, *"...but those who hope in the LORD will renew their strength. They will soar on wings like eagles; they will run and not grow weary."*

How are you feeling today? Are you feeling paralysed, stopped in your tracks by defeat and depression?

When we feel low, we can often self-medicate in a way that is unhelpful, which leads to a cycle of despising ourselves further. I am praying that instead you will choose attitudes and make choices that will bless you and make you well.

I am praying for you, even as you read this, that you know God next to you in your darkness; that you have a glimmer of hope that life will one day be brighter for you. I believe this with all my heart.

Why?

Because there is an edict that has been written about you in Heaven that declares that God will use ALL things to work together for your good, not just the easy things (see Romans 8:28). Not just the things you understand. Not just the happy, shiny things. All things ... because His plan is to prosper you (see Jeremiah 29:11).

Prospering us means to make us rich in wisdom and discernment. I have learnt that I can't be rich in wisdom unless I experience something where wisdom is needed.

I have realised that I can't be an overcomer until I have overcome something.

So God will provide me with an opportunity to learn those lessons. Perhaps this is what you are facing right this very moment.

How is that going?

I am praying that God will hold you tight and give you the energy you need to read on.

One of the ways I try and combat negative thinking in my

heart is very simple. I imagine that my mind is a large bucket or bin. If I put poor thoughts and rotten ideas into that bin, it will start to smell and leak into other areas of my life. It will pollute my mind further. It will also be fairly toxic for other people and start to bleed into their lives as well.

What we think about and what we cultivate in our heads and hearts really matters.

What is in that bin of yours? Does it need emptying?

So many of us struggle with untrained minds and a cycle of unhelpful thinking. We think that we can't remember all that we need to, that our minds are chaotic and as though they are at war with us. This is a classic tool of the enemy. He badly wants us to feel as though we are overwhelmed and underachieving.

Perhaps we feel as though we are often wasting time and failing to finish important tasks. Feeling unworthy and less able than those around us will heighten our sense of discouragement. If you have a "to do" list that only grows and doesn't ever diminish you have a problem! Not achieving even simple tasks will deepen any sense of disrespect we have for ourselves.

You may not be aware of this, but feeling as though you have a bad memory or poor capacity is one of the main weapons the enemy uses to attack your self-image. He loves it when we look at the day and already feel defeated and small. But there is good news! God has given us sufficient and efficient minds to do all He has called us to do.

One of my favourite power verses in the Bible is 2 Timothy 1:7 (NKJV) It says this:

"For God has not given us a spirit of fear, but of power and

of love and of a sound mind."

If you are battling today to feel as though your mind is secure and sound, say this verse as a declaration over it! If you are looking at a seemingly impossible list of things you want to achieve, say this verse over yourself. You do not need to be afraid. Look what God has given you! He has given you POWER, LOVE and a SOUND MIND. Some versions of scripture translate this last phrase as self–discipline. Is this lacking in your life?

Ask God for it. He longs to help you.

HEALTH WORRIES

The most familiar of all the Psalms in the Bible starts with a small but significant phrase:

"The Lord is my shepherd; I shall not want." (Psalm 23:1)

For some of us, the word "want" is a bit tricky right now. It is a season where many of us are wanting something … very badly. The Bible is very clear here. It says you and I need to decide something. We need to speak something out and say something over our lives.

If you and I believe that the Lord is our Shepherd (and I very much do) then we should also believe that it is possible to say (and mean): I SHALL NOT WANT. In other words,

I will lack nothing of value.

I won't need anything I don't have.

I won't be without.

I will be provided for.

I will be sorted.

I will be OK.

I will be blessed.

It will be well.

Humanly speaking we will always want something. It may be a material thing like a new car or a laptop, but I am not talking about possessions here. I am thinking more about what we "possess" in a deeper sense.

If you were honest with yourself what would be on your list today?

Better health?

A closer friend?

A better relationship with someone in your family?

A child?

Greater financial stability?

A closer walk with God?

Those things are all reasonable and wholesome desires in some ways, but sometimes those wants can allow us to think negatively and sow dissatisfaction into our days.

We can blame God that we do not have what we feel we need NOW. We can tell Him, very loudly, that He is not ALL we want. That we *want* MORE. That we *need* MORE.

Let me tell you something about the way I think God sees things.

If God gives me vision for something like loving a tough person, writing a new book or praying in a new way then He will give me PROvision for that vision. If He gives you the vision of getting healed, then He will PROvide for that vision in His way and in His time.

He is a PRO!!!

He has the best CV of anyone I know or will ever know.

He has a 100% faithful track record and He will never lose His reputation or His marbles or His power.

He is a PROtector, a PROvider, and a PROducer.

What. He. Says. Happens.

Our desire or our healing may not come as instantly as we hope, or be wrapped up in the way we thought. But it will come.

Sewn into your vision (which God gave you anyway) is His PRO-vision for that vision to happen.

So if He told you that you would one day run your own company, you will. If He told you that you would begin to change how you feel about your past, you will. If He told you that you will be well, you will get well. But it starts with a declaration from you. You need to say the following words:

"The Lord is my shepherd, I shall not want."

So are you ready to say that over your soul today?

What we speak out has real power.

A couple of years ago my friend Debra Green spoke about the fact that before her beloved Mum died, she had told Debra she would one day be awarded an OBE. That hope has, of course, since come into being. I have often wondered how much of that was because Debra may have started to think differently about her own career path and her life choices, from that moment on.

The Bible says, *"...No good thing will He withhold from those who walk uprightly"* (Psalms 84:11 NKJV). Believe for and speak out for your inner and outer healing today.

GRIEF OR LOSS

Perhaps you are struggling with your security because you are currently suffering from grief or loss. I write about this extensively in my book *Good Grief – living through loss* and

I encourage you to get hold of a copy. It will help you to understand more about how to strengthen yourself through this hard time.

Grief is one of the reasons we can lose confidence in ourselves. The loss of a person, job or a relationship can leave us feeling at sea and desperately insecure. We can lose ourselves in that season and only God (with the aid of His people) can help us through.

Psalm 31:9-10 has been very helpful to me in my own grief. It says this:

"Be gracious to me, O Lord, for I am in distress; my eye is wasted from grief; my soul and my body also. For my life is spent with sorrow, and my years with sighing; my strength fails..."

When I was in a period of mourning I felt as though I wasting away and that my own life had somehow come to an end. I felt weak, tired and as though I had no energy. But God was gracious to me in my distress. He understood every part of my pain and the fears that were rife in my spirit.

So many passages from the Bible comforted me and I would encourage you to make a habit of looking them up. Put them somewhere you can see and read them on a daily basis.

IN SUMMARY

There are many reasons why we can struggle with insecurity and I hope that some of the things I have covered in this chapter have spoken to you and helped you.

Whether you were brought up unhelpfully or have gone through tragedy, whether you have had a lack of love and acceptance from others, or have been bullied or hurt in some way, I pray that you are able to leave those situations in the hands of our Loving God. I pray that He will give you the things you are hoping and praying for right now. But that means you have to do something too. Psalm 37:4 NKJV says: *"Delight yourself...in the Lord, and He shall give you the desires of your heart."*

Delighting yourself in God means not delighting in yourself. It means trusting in Him when you want to trust no one. It means giving your life to Him when you'd prefer to keep it to yourself. Can you do that?

You see, you are good enough and able enough to do all Jesus wants you to, whether you are qualified, popular, gifted, favoured or the exact opposite. HE is your security. You don't need the approval of any of your family or your friends – although it's great when you have it. You don't need the advice of your boss or your colleagues. All you really need is God's words over you.

Some while ago a member of our small group shared with us about some interviews he had conducted at work to fill a management position. Whilst many CVs had come across well on paper, every person he had interviewed was rather a disappointment in person.

Feeling more than a little disconsolate, he was not very pleased to receive a recommendation about a totally unsuitable-sounding woman from a colleague. He listened to her lack of experience, coupled with the fact that she was deaf, and wondered why this lady was wasting his time. More to humour the member of staff concerned, he wearily agreed to see the person in question. Within seconds of the interview he realised he had, at long last, found his dream manager. On paper she was a disaster, but in person she was dynamite.

You are able to do all He has planned for you. You never need to utter the phrase,

"I am not good enough."

Because you are.

Truth from this chapter:
We can miss beauty right in front of us
We can be cast down by the world we inhabit
We can see other people's success as our apparent failure.
Honouring others is vital for our own inner security.
God can help us cope with our weaknesses and honour Him with our strengths
Failure is an event not a person
God takes great delight in you.
His opinion of you is what truly matters.
The Bible will tell us what God thinks of us.
FEAR is the same thing as worship.
The fear of God makes us strong and keeps us strong!
You are able to do all He has planned for you

4
In Security

[why we don't need to feel insecure]

"And you will feel secure, because there is hope; you will look around and take your rest in security." (Job 11:18 ESV)

German psychoanalyst Eric Fromm said, "The task we must set for ourselves is not to feel secure, but to be able to tolerate insecurity."

I couldn't agree less.

This is not what God wants for us at all. Tolerating our weaknesses isn't any way to live!

God doesn't want us to go through life feeling content with not feeling content. He wants more for us than that.

As we have already said, any self-help book will tell you to "believe in yourself". Or, perhaps more abstractly, to "be the best you that you can be". On the surface those sentiments sound fine, but the problem is that they rely on *you* to be the answer to your own problem. We all know that is a flawed model. If you are having a bad day, or month or even year, the chances are this won't work for you. You can't pull yourself out of a hole without help.

We will all let ourselves down. We will promise ourselves something but go back on it. We cannot always depend on ourselves. You and I need to believe in something or rather in *someone* who will never fail us or let us down. You and I need to believe in *God in us*.

I looked up how many times the phrase "IN Christ" is used in the Bible. Just in the letters that Paul wrote, the tally is a staggering 165. God is trying to show us something here! Our security and our identity is meant to be found IN HIM and in Him alone.

I know this isn't easy. I know it goes against what many of us have been taught about "looking after number 1", but I totally promise you that this is the way to lasting personal security.

REJECTION

One of the main problems that stands in the way of us feeling secure, is the powerful and unsightly emotion of rejection. All of us will face some level of rejection in life. I don't know who you have felt rejected by – maybe a girlfriend, or a business partner, or a university, or a family member? Some of us have been through terrible situations where it can feel as though life itself is against us. The Latin noun *rēicere*, which means "to throw back," is the derivation of the word *rejection*. Rejection can make us feel as though someone has picked us up and hurled us away, like rubbish.

Rejection robs us of relationship with others because it makes us afraid. It causes us to put up defences and barricade ourselves in, and others out. Rejection can leave us broken and insecure. It can also cause us to lash out at others or withdraw completely.

But do you know that in Jesus you will find someone who could never and will never reject you?

Romans 8:38-39 (AMP) says:

"For I am convinced [and continue to be convinced – beyond any doubt] that neither death, nor life, nor angels, nor principalities, nor things present and threatening, nor things to come, nor powers, nor height, nor depth, nor any other created thing, will be able to separate us from the [unlimited] love of God, which is in Christ Jesus our Lord"

Nothing can stand in the way of the unlimited love of God which, guess what? Is IN Jesus.

One of my favourite characters in the whole of the Bible is the wonderful person of Hannah. She is a praying, trusting woman who makes a tremendous promise of sacrifice when she cries out to God for a baby boy. She is a fabulous example of someone who finds her security in God alone, even after being rejected by a member of her own family.

Let's read together a small part of the passage where she is praising God for answering her many prayers.

"The Lord has filled my heart with joy;
I feel very strong in the Lord.
I can laugh at my enemies;
I am glad because you have helped me!
There is no one holy like the Lord.
There is no God but you;
there is no Rock like our God." (1 Samuel 2:1-10 NCV)

I find this passage really interesting. She is not finding her security in the answer to her prayer – her baby – but in the God who gave her the baby in the first place. This is something we can sometimes forget to do. In the joy of the "answered prayer moment" we can be tempted to put our securities into our answered prayer itself – the new job, our new baby or our abilities and talents.

Hannah chooses to look at her life differently. She praises God for filling her heart with joy. She speaks over herself that she is now strong and secure enough to laugh at those who scorned her. She has learnt not to praise the gift, but the giver.

There is an old hymn that my Grandma used to sing to me that began with the line, "Praise God from whom all blessings flow…"

It is so vital that we truly understand that our blessings come from God and that He is worthy of our thanks and praise.

ROOTS OF REJECTION

It is helpful to understand where our rejection comes from in order that we can give it to God and allow Him to take it from us. Rejection of any kind is an ugly plant with deeply unattractive roots. It is a fast-growing weed that can grow rampantly if left unchecked. Perhaps, though not exclusively, rejection can manifest itself in the following ways:

1. Anger

Over the years I have sat and prayed with many people. One of the most common out-workings of rejection is seen in anger. Perhaps the person might be angry with themselves, or project that onto others, or God. Holding on to anger is dangerous for us. It is a toxic and damaging incendiary device that can blow up in our faces. Proverbs 29:22 tells us that, *"An angry person stirs up conflict, and a hot-tempered person commits many sins."* Anger bubbles away under the surface and can rise up at a time when we least expect it. If you find yourself getting irrationally angry about something or someone, ask God what is going on. Seek out a good friend to pray with you about it. It may be a root of deeper rejection that you need to identify and deal with.

When I was a primary school teacher I once taught in a very rough school with some really volatile pupils. I asked permission of the Head-teacher to write and deliver some Anger Management classes with some of the more challenging children. They did not know why they felt angry. It took a number of sessions to identify a sad truth. Time after time they had been let down or rejected by those who were meant to be caring for them. Anger often has its roots in rejection.

2. Bitterness

Maybe our rejection comes out in bitterness or an unwillingness to forgive ourselves, or others. I once knew someone who was so bitter inside that whenever someone hurt him or offended him he wrote it on a "post-it" note and displayed it on his wall. The wall became a list of reasons he could stay bitter. He wanted to remember the hurt and remind himself of it.

Many of us will do this too, but in more subtle ways. Whenever someone says something nice to us we won't hear it because we will mentally read the post-it notes of bitterness in our heads. We will see that years ago someone said or did the opposite of that. So we can't "hear" the compliment.

Bitterness spoils everything we have. It poisons goodness and love and hope. God knows the damage it can cause and how lasting that damage is. Ephesians 4:31 (AMP) says,

"Let all bitterness and wrath and anger and clamour [perpetual animosity, resentment, strife, fault-finding] and slander be put away from you, along with every kind of malice [all spitefulness, verbal abuse, malevolence]."

Is this something God is showing you about your own past today? Isn't it time you laid down those things that are causing you to remember the sins of others?

3. Rebellion

Often rejection will take us on a journey towards a lack of trust in others. We will become much more independent and display stubbornness or selfishness. We might be stalwart "copers" and not good at asking for help, even when we are desperate inside. Perhaps we will go the other way and go out of our way to rebel and make life difficult for others to somehow "pay the world back" for what it has done to us. 1 Samuel 15:23 (NCV) is very clear about how God sees such things:

"For rebellion is as bad as the sin of witchcraft, and stubbornness is as bad as worshiping idols."

That is a pretty hefty verse! But I have included it on purpose. Our Heavenly fFather knows the destructive power of rebellion. He understands that it can cause us to not trust in Him or in His people and He wants it gone from our lives. Our stubbornness and refusal to admit that we need help, or are wrong, can become an idol. Lets search our hearts and make sure they are clean.

4. Defensiveness

Another root of rejection may manifest itself in us becoming overly critical, exercising harsh judgement over ourselves or others. Many people coping with rejection feel they have to try harder and be more successful than others. They put excess pressure on themselves to achieve, but maintain distance from others, trying to build up their own sense of worth by being critical of other people. Those who struggle in this area make hard task-masters. They are aggressive or defensive towards people and can be quick to take offence.

God wants us to leave the judging of others to Him and concentrate on our own lives.

Romans 14:10 (AMP) says:

"But you, why do you criticise your brother? Or you again, why do you look down on your [believing] brother or regard him with contempt? For we will all stand before the judgement seat of God [who alone is judge]."

I think I was born critical. I probably gave my own birth a strong 9 out of 10! I always have an opinion about an event, a service, or a person. I have had to learn that some of that critical thinking is of God. Striving for excellence and wanting things to be effective and efficient is a good thing. But sometimes I have been too critical of things and that has the capacity to be destructive.

Take care that when you are commenting, your heart is to improve things and not make yourself look more competent, important or able.

4. Self-pity

Maybe rejection will cause us to feel self-pity. We will remind ourselves of the pain we are in and replay all that has happened to get us to that point. We will wake up going through the same thought processes each day and feel static, or even worse, as though we are going backwards emotionally. Self-pity causes us to take our eyes off the goodness of God and focus fully on what we don't know, or don't have.

Jeremiah 15:19 (AMP) says:

"Therefore, thus says the Lord [to Jeremiah], 'If you repent [and give up this mistaken attitude of despair and self-pity], then I will restore you [to a state of inner peace]. So that you may stand before Me [as My obedient representative].'"

I don't know about you but I love having a state of inner peace. That means anything can happen to me or around me and I can withstand it. Self -pity means we can be easily knocked. We are so focused inward that our eyes aren't open or looking up.

Imagine for a moment that you are standing in a room alone. Someone creeps into the room but you don't see them because you have your eyes shut and are thinking about yourself. If they tried to knock you over and overpower you, you would be an easy target. You are not watching out for them and you have your eyes focused on yourself. Self-pity is that dangerous. It makes you vulnerable to attack.

If you are battling with self-pity today, ask God to reveal the root of that rejection in you. Ask Him to show you who to forgive and to open your eyes to all the goodness around you.

5. Escapism

This root of rejection takes many forms. It can manifest itself in addictions like pornography, over-eating, alcohol or drug abuse or in developing other habits to comfort ourselves such as excessive spending.

Some people also find the need to physically leave a stressful situation, walking out on their families due to previous or current rejection. Others will try to bury their problems in work, sport, sex or even, in the case of one lady I knew, obsessive cleaning.

We can try and look for a way to mask the problem. But the problem will remain undealt with. One of my friends had damp in his basement. He tried to treat it with a special paint, but the damp just came back. Why? Because he had tried to treat it from the outside, but he hadn't tackled the inside. He painted over it rather than pulling it out. He was looking at the rot, but not the root of the rot.

We can often do the same. We can think, "I wish I could give up smoking!" without tackling the reason we started smoking in the first place.

Zechariah 10:2 (NLV) says something so profound about escapism:

"The false gods say what is not true. Those who use their secret ways tell lies about the false dreams they have seen. Their comfort means nothing. So the people go from place to place like sheep and are troubled because they have no shepherd."

The trouble is that if we look for comfort outside of God, we will keep looking. It is an expensive, personally costly waste of energy, time and emotion. We will end up singing a song like the famous U2 one that says, "I still haven't found what I'm looking for."

GOOD NEWS!

I don't know how you felt as you read through that last section. Perhaps one or more of those roots resonates with you and you feel you need to take some time out to pray through them. Please don't read on until you have made peace with God about how you are feeling.

The good news is that we don't have to live in or act out of rejection. Sometimes we may feel as though we must do certain things in order to be loved by God, but this simply isn't true. He has given us all the tools we need to break the power of rejection and stop any of its roots from taking a hold over us.

Elizabeth Elliot wrote, "Where does your security lie? Is God your refuge, your hiding place, your stronghold, your shepherd, your counsellor, your friend, your redeemer, your saviour, your guide? If He is, you don't need to search any further for security."

Before we go any further, if God isn't those things for you; if you don't feel that He is your refuge, your hiding place, your stronghold, your shepherd, your counsellor, your friend, your redeemer, your saviour, or your guide, then you can ask Him to be those things for you now. Don't go another moment or another day without asking Him to be that for you. You don't need to try on your own any more! He is waiting with open arms to greet you, love you and bless you. What's more He will cause you to be a blessing to others. If you want to, you can stop with me now and just pray this prayer:

Dear Lord Jesus,
Thank you that you love me. Thank you that your love for me has no strings attached. You know that I have tried to live

my life without you and its not gone so well. Today, in this moment I give you all I am and all I hope to be. I offer you my past and my present and my future and ask that you would be my friend and my helper. Please forgive me for every time I have tried to go it alone or make my own happiness. Please take the weight of the mistakes I have made and transform my life into one that pleases you and blesses others. Amen.

If you prayed that prayer, WELL DONE! Let me encourage you to find a local church and tell someone there. Another great step that will help you is to go on an Alpha course or a course such as "Freedom in Christ". Many churches will advertise that they run such courses on their websites.

There are a number of practical things you can do to help yourself stay in a place of security in God and these can be found in chapter 6.

BUILDING A BRIDGE

Recently my husband and I celebrated our 15th wedding anniversary. As a surprise I got one of my brothers to book us a trip to New York where one of my other brothers is currently living.

We had the most wonderful time with Dan and his wife, Sam. It was the trip of a lifetime and we spent precious family time with them both. One day they took us to an amazing restaurant for a meal overlooking the Manhattan skyline and then we all walked over the Brooklyn Bridge. It is an amazing feat of engineering and I loved the unusual structure of it.

I have since discovered that the bridge was started by an engineer called John Roebling and that its unique design was his idea. Roebling realised that hemp rope was both expensive and easily broken and so began producing wire rope in 1841 to use in hauling goods along canals. He understood that wire rope led to all sorts of building possibilities. In 1841 he started work on what is now called the Brooklyn Bridge spanning the East River in New York.

Tragically, one day in 1869 he was standing at the edge of a dock, working on the location where the bridge would be built, when his foot was crushed by a docking ferry. His injured toes had to be amputated. He refused further medical treatment and wanted to cure his foot by what was known as "water therapy" (the practice of pouring water over the wound). His condition deteriorated and he succumbed to tetanus 24 days after the accident.

But he had started something amazing. He had opened up the possibility that someone could build a bridge from Manhattan to Brooklyn. Experts thought it was an impossibility. They said a bridge spanning that distance couldn't withstand the great force of the winds and the tides of the river. But Roebling refused to listen. His idea led his son, Washington, and his daughter-in-law, Emily, to continue to work on the bridge.

Washington was named chief engineer after his father's death in mid-1869. He made several important improvements to the bridge design and further developed bridge building techniques. But in 1870, another tragedy struck the process. Fire broke out on the bridge and, in his efforts to put it out, Washington suffered from terrible compression sickness. This shattered his health and made him unable to visit the site or lead the build as he had before. The prevailing wisdom was to abandon the project, but Washington Roebling was determined to fulfil his father's dream. Whilst his illness meant that he could not walk or talk easily, he developed a system of communication by touching his wife's arm with a finger, and she in turn conveyed his ideas to the project engineers. Emily took it upon herself to learn bridge construction, became his nurse, companion and confidante and took over much of the chief engineer's duties, including day-to-day supervision and project management. For thirteen years that's how they slowly worked together. In 1883 the first car drove over the bridge! In spite of death, fire and all the nay-saying, that family continued to build.

Their bridge is now a triumph of engineering and a powerful symbol of how people unselfishly overcame adversity.

I loved finding out about that incredible family and their story. I love the fact that they refused to let the past determine their future. They chose to build a bridge and millions of people are so grateful that they did.

Can you imagine if they had let the rejection of people's words persuade them to stop? They could have easily given up when John died, but they chose to work hard for something they believed in. It was just one finger on the arm of that lady that told her what to do and where to build.

Do you know that God can do the same for you?

He can reach out His hand towards you and guide you one step at a time.

If you are currently facing a seemingly impossible situation, I hope you can take comfort from this incredible story. God can help us to do the most unlikely and impossible things.

Luke 6:43-45 (MSG) says that: *"You don't get wormy apples*

off a healthy tree, nor good apples off a diseased tree. The health of the apple tells the health of the tree. You must begin with your own life-giving lives. It's who you are, not what you say and do, that counts. Your true being brims over into true words and deeds."

God can bring the good out of us if we let Him. I believe He has hidden His dreams in you and He wants you to fulfill them. You can be secure that no matter what happens to you and to those around you, His purposes will prevail and healthy fruit will come.

You see, God's views of us are:

- Independently verified – He doesn't need a reference from anyone else.
- Not changeable – He won't rethink His answers.
- Accurate – He can't be wrong.
- Unbiased – He isn't swayed by others.
- Soul deep – He looks at the inside of us.
- Not based on comparison – He doesn't look at us in the light of how others are performing.

Just read that list again! It's truly staggering when we really grasp the truth of the fact that God isn't motivated by selfish ambition. He doesn't take offence, feel disappointment, or get moody with us. He is not quick to anger, slow to forgive, nor does He keep a long, ugly list of all our failings. The Bible reminds us of something we often forget which is this:

"God is not human, that he should lie, not a human being, that he should change his mind." (Numbers 23:19)

There are many times in our lives when we get caught up in a wrong opinion of God. We start to imagine Him with flawed human characteristics and treat Him as though He is disappointed with us; angry, distant, or fed up. But God cannot act in those petulant, childish ways. We often project our ideas of what He might be thinking and feeling onto Him as if He were a mere human. We must remember that He is GOD!

God will not change His mind about you or me. He loves us whether we are lovable or not. He loves us whether we love Him back, or not. He loves us because He is God and He made us as His children. Once we understand that, we never need to be insecure again.

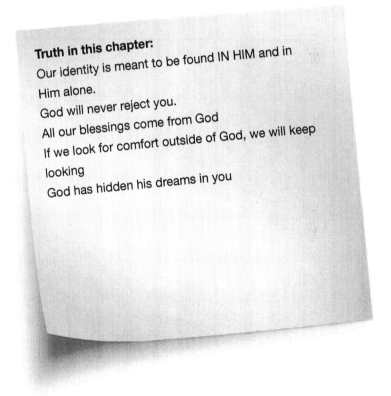

Truth in this chapter:
Our identity is meant to be found IN HIM and in Him alone.
God will never reject you.
All our blessings come from God
If we look for comfort outside of God, we will keep looking
God has hidden his dreams in you

5
Security Guard

[how to live securely]

"Let Him tell you you're worth wanting, loving, even liking, pursuing, fighting for, and, yes, beloved, keeping." – Beth Moore

A huge part of being secure is understanding how valuable you are to God. I think many of us find this difficult. It is an especially British trait to have a low self-image and to put ourselves down.

THROWING OUT THE RUBBISH

The story is told of a cleaning woman at an Italian gallery who accidentally threw away thousand of dollars of art by New York modernist Paul Branca. She mistook his crumpled newspaper, cardboard, and biscuit crumbs installation scattered across the floor, for rubbish. The pieces, estimated to be worth around $15,000, were apparently intended to make viewers think about the environment.

They certainly made the cleaner think about her environment!

She bundled them up and put them in a bin-bag.

Whoops!

I think she should be forgiven for this one! I would have done the same in her shoes. Sometimes people don't understand what is valuable to others.

For example, did you know that old cereal is valuable? It's true! In 1988 an American cereal company called Ralston released a new product called the Nintendo Cereal System. I'm not sure how you can have a system for breakfast cereal, but that's what they called it. Anyway, it was designed in a box that came with two different, rather ambiguous flavours of cereal – a Mario Brothers themed "Fruity" one and a Zelda themed "Berry" cereal.

This 27-year-old vintage cereal is now considered one of the most attractive purchases for die-hard cereal collectors out there. (Perhaps, like me, you are still coming to terms with that being an actual thing?) Did you know that an unopened box of this treat recently netted just over $200? So keep your Shreddies people! In the future they could be part of your pension!

COLLECTABLES

I find it amazing the things that people collect. Seemingly worthless things can be given credence and value. I have the strange habit of collecting antique cutlery. If you ask me why I get excited about old forks, I am at a loss. I just love them but I can't really explain it.

God is a collector too.

Matthew 10:29-30 in the Living Bible version says this:

"Not one sparrow (What do they cost? Two for a penny?)

can fall to the ground without your Father knowing it. And the very hairs of your head are all numbered."

God doesn't collect stamps or even sparrows. He doesn't have a prize-winning giant vegetable collection or a worrying amount of One Direction memorabilia. What He prizes is far more valuable than vintage stale cereal too.

The word "valuable" is a translation of the Latin word *carus* which means "dear" in English. But its original meaning is "costly, expensive, or high-priced". Is this how you would speak about yourself? Because it is how God would describe you.

How much are you worth? What value would you place on yourself? How irreplaceable would you say you are? I'm not talking about money here. We can sometimes confuse self-worth with financial worth, but they are very different.

Your value has nothing to do with your *valuables*. It is not about how many bedrooms your house has, or whether the diamonds in your ears are from Boots or Boodles. It's not about which car you drive or what you own. It's about how valuable YOU are.

TRILLION DOLLAR MAN

We measure our value poorly. We can also remind ourselves of situations where others did not treat us well and so think we are somehow worth less than we are. But this is not true. We are hugely valuable. In fact, I have good news for you! In hard cash terms, you are worth over a thousand pounds!

What I do I mean? Well, you have a huge variety of elements in your body. Amongst other things these are made up of:

Oxygen

Carbon

Hydrogen

Nitrogen

Calcium

Phosphorus

Potassium

Sulphur

Sodium

Chlorine

Magnesium

Iron

According to current conversion rates, if you sold them all you would net about £1224.72 – based on your weight. (Some of us are worth a bit more! Just saying!)

But actually this is not what you are really worth at all.

If you calculate the cost of *creating* each cell in your body, it would be about *six thousand trillion dollars*. I couldn't work out the conversion of that. Let's just say that £1000000000000 US Dollars equals £676786890000.00 British Pounds Sterling. In other words you are utterly and totally priceless!

Look at your hands and your feet, look at your eyes and your skin. Everything has been designed and made to function and work for a purpose. But of course we are more than bodies and a random collection of elements. We are, more importantly, souls too.

The Bible tells us time and time again that we are valuable to God. So what makes us so valuable? Well like the rubbish installation and the antique cereal, we are actually worth what someone will pay. You are worth what someone is willing to pay for you.

THE BIG SPENDER

Imagine you were a gazillionaire. What would you choose to spend your money on?

Well on sale today you could have:

Britain's Most Expensive Parking Space – going for a mere £400,000 under the Royal Albert Hall.

Or perhaps if you were a little peckish, you could Pop over to New York and order yourself a Bellissima pizza in Nino's – yours for a small fee of only $1000.

You could treat yourself to the worlds most expensive cup of tea with a PG tips diamond tea bag. Yours for the eye-watering price tag of only $14000.

People are crazy, aren't they?!

God is the richest person who has ever existed or will ever exist and do you know what He chose to do with His riches, with His wisdom and His knowledge? He didn't waste them on trinkets and jewels. He chose to spend them on YOU.

God, Jesus and the Holy Spirit operate in a kind of investment business. They are partners whose sole aim is to get the most stock that they can. And that stock includes you.

In Luke 15 Jesus tells three stories – the lost son, the lost coin and the lost sheep. It's the same meaning in each story. Jesus is saying, "You are valuable to me! Your life has meaning and purpose. Because of this I will go looking for you if you get lost. I love you."

I will look more at the story of the lost son later in this chapter.

You matter to God. Let's have a look at why.

INTRICATE DETAIL

The passage we read earlier tells us that, *"Not one sparrow can fall to the ground without your Father knowing it. And the very hairs of our heads are all numbered."*

What does this tell us about God?

It shows us His minute attention to detail.

In the Bible 2 sparrows were worth less than a penny. And yet God cares for them and knows their destiny.

More than this, He is aware of something that *we* wouldn't say mattered at all. Knowing that we *have* hair might matter to us. Knowing the number of hairs? Less so!

On the average head there are over one hundred thousand strands of hair. And God knows all that about you. Instantly. This means He also knows if you're in love with someone, if you haven't slept well, if you have a secret addiction to daytime telly, if you need a good cry, if you're just checking Him out to see if He's real, if you despise Stilton ... in fact, everything about you.

Why? Because He sees our value.

But perhaps we don't feel this way about ourselves?

THE BATTLE FOR SIGNIFICANCE

Part of the reason may be that we have an enemy who doesn't want us to think we are valuable at all. So every thought that he puts into our minds is about us not mattering; about people not loving us or valuing us. The devil's job is to make us feel insignificant. And he is quite good at it.

Or maybe others have hurt us and told us negative things.

One boyfriend I had told me I wasn't allowed to go to a certain party with him because it was only for "pretty girls". He reminded me that he was only going out with me because I was "funny". I just let him say that to me! I believed him. Now, I would give him a significant punch – in the Lord, of course.

Do you sometimes feel worthless? Or, at times, have you been slighted or treated as though you were of little value?

I think these verses give us a clue about how to feel about ourselves. If the cheapest birds on earth matter to God, then those that the world sees as unimportant or valueless matter to Him too. The truth is that everyone matters, from the richest to the poorest, from the oldest to the youngest. All of us are valuable to God.

VALUED

What about if we are feeling worthless and struggling in the midst of those kinds of emotions? Perhaps we need to remind ourselves how much God values us. As you already know, I love an acronym! So to help us understand how God sees us, I've created one for the word valued. It is this:

Valid

Accepted

Loved

Unique

Expensive

Desirable

This is how God sees you!

You are **V**alid – Isaiah 44:2 God says *"You were in my care before you were born."* You have a right to be here. Your life has validity and value and purpose. Whatever the circumstances of your conception or birth, you were intended.

You are **A**ccepted – Ephesians 1:5 says you were *"predestined for adoption."* God chose you before you chose Him. He accepts you as you are. You don't have to change in order for God to adopt you and want you in His family.

You are **L**oved – Romans 5:8 says, *"God shows his love for us in this, whilst we were still sinners, Christ died for us."* Nothing we can do will stop God loving us.

You are **U**nique – God speaks over you that you are *"fearfully and wonderfully made."* He designed you specifically and He enjoys who you are (see Psalm 139:13-16).

You are **E**xpensive – 1 Corinthians 6:19 says you were *"bought with a price."* We are not cheap imitations found on some crummy market stall. We are designer goods, made to last forever.

You are **D**esirable – Ephesians 1:13 tells us that we are *"God's own possession."* He desires us. He wants us. We have value.

ASKING THE WRONG QUESTION

The search for self worth and value has puzzled generations of people for thousands of years. It's been the question at the root of poems, songs and countless books. That's because we typically begin at the wrong place – we begin by looking at ourselves. We ask self-centered questions like, "What do I want to be? What should I do with my life? What are my goals and my ambitions? What are my dreams for my future?" But focusing on ourselves will never reveal our life's purpose or our value. The Bible says, *"It is God who directs the lives of his creatures; everyone's life is in his power"* (see Job 12:10). To find our worth and our value, we must begin with God, our Creator, and His reasons for creating us. When we grasp that we were made *by* God and *for* God, so much of life will begin to make sense.

It is only in God that we discover where we came from and where we will end up. In Him we can see our reason for being alive, our identity, our significance, and our destiny. As Colossians 1:16 (MSG) says:

"For everything, absolutely everything, above and below, visible and invisible ... everything got started in him and finds its purpose in him."

If you have felt as though something is lacking in your life and you are wondering what your purpose is, but you have done that outside of looking to God. Bingo! There is your answer. You need to find your purpose in Him.

TO DIE FOR

You may have heard people use an expression like "This ice cream is to die for." They don't literally mean that they love their *Häagen-Dazs* so much they are happy to lie down in front of the nearest motor vehicle just for a quick lick of it. We know that it's just an expression that means, "This ice cream is fairly good quality and I am really rather enjoying it." But Jesus uses the same phrase about you and actually MEANS every word of it. You are TO DIE FOR. Do you know that Jesus spilt His own blood in order for you to be made right with God? He sees you as priceless and more than worth dying for. So do you treat yourself as though you are?

The story is told of a brother and sister who cleaned out

their Mum's house following her death. They found an old vase in the attic and whilst they didn't much like it, they decided to have it valued.

They were pretty excited when they were told it was worth between £800,000 and £1.2m. However, at auction, no one expected the reaction from some Chinese buyers who pushed the bidding up to a staggering £43m. Two Chinese businessmen got into a bidding war and the price kept going higher and higher.

The 18th century Qianlong-dynasty porcelain piece eventually fetched £53 million. Imagine that! They could have thrown that vase away or given it to a charity shop!

Like that vase, you are worth what someone is willing to pay for you. You might not think you are that valuable, but you have been auctioned and God has put in a crazily high and outrageous bid for you. No matter what others have said about you or to you, you are valuable to Him and He wants you.

THE ELDER BROTHER

Many of us find it hard to come to terms with this kind of love. We simply don't feel worthy of it. The following story is my take on the famous passage in the Bible about the prodigal son in Luke 15. But I have written it from the point of view of the elder brother. I think as a character, he is a fascinating example of someone who did not feel secure, valued or loved.

I suggest you make yourself a drink and put your feet up while you read this:

"He's always been the same. Ever since he was little, Joe has craved attention. He's a party animal, a real big mouth.

Sometimes we got on, but the older he got, the more he wanted the company of his friends rather than to stay at home with us. We drifted apart because, well, he was a drifter. One minute he was best friends with this guy, and the following week it was someone else.

I have had the same set of friends all my life. We do everything together – the three of us. But Joe, he always has someone new to know. Something new to try. He gets bored easily does my little brother.

When Mum got sick, Joe was hardly there. He said he didn't have the stomach for the nursing. I found that ... really hard – after all she'd done for him ... but he was in and out the door each day in a few minutes. He never sat with her or just let her talk. When she died there was a knot in my stomach that stayed for years. I found it hard to talk about her, but I knew I would always, always stay on the farm. I wanted to do it for her. I didn't want her to worry. I wanted her to know she could count on me. That Dad could count on me. I was dependable, trustworthy. I turned up and worked hard and always did what needed doing. I wanted her to be proud. I wanted Dad to be proud. That's who I am. I am someone you can rely on.

But Joe ... Joe is different. One day we were in the fields as usual, planting. It was back-breaking work and Joe skived off early. He said he was meeting one of his friends for a drink. But that's not what he did. He went to one of my best friends houses and started getting friendly with his sister, if you know what I mean. There were rumours and we had to try and quosh them. I warned him, but Joe isn't a listener. He is a talker, a shouter. He laughed at me and called me old fashioned.

"When are you going to have a bit of fun David? Lighten up! Enjoy life. You are always working! You're old before your time!" he'd said, his face twisted with disgust.

I nearly punched him, but he ran off, laughing. I seethed for weeks.

Then one day, out of the blue, he came in with this funny smile on his face as though he'd had the best idea ever. He whispered something to Dad. Dad's face fell. I just knew he had said something awful. But Dad wouldn't tell me what it was. As Joe left, Dad seemed preoccupied and sad.

Later on that morning I confronted my little brother.

"What have you said to Dad?" I asked him.

"Oh, not much." Joe smiled nonchalantly, "I just asked him if I could have my share of the estate now. No point waiting any longer, is there? I mean, I am missing all the fun."

I couldn't believe it. Joe was basically asking Dad for his inheritance. He was saying, "I wish you were dead so I could have all your money!" I couldn't believe he had said it.

But my little brother had already mentally packed his bags. He was leaving that day with his pockets full and his father's emptier than they were. I tried to hold my tongue as I watched him leave. But I couldn't

"Why did you give it to him Dad?" I said. "You could have withheld it and told him he had to wait!"

"He would have left without my blessing," said Dad, slowly. "And that would have been worse than him leaving at all." Those words stung my heart and my eyes swam with tears. It wasn't fair.

I remember lying awake for hours that night with very

mixed emotions. In some ways I was glad he was gone. He was such hard work to have around. He didn't pull his weight on the farm and was always trying to get out of work. At least without him we could take on a couple of hired hands who would actually do what we needed, and properly. But I knew Dad was broken hearted.

The night after Joe had gone, I found him on the roof of the house sitting in the darkness. He was waiting for Joe.

"He's not coming back Dad," I said. "He needs to do this. He's never been happy here. And maybe we will be better off without him."

Dad looked at me sadly, touched my hand and smiled. He didn't say anything ... I couldn't tell what he was thinking.

Dad was very quiet for a few days and the farm seemed to be quiet too. I thought I would like it, but I did sort of miss the drama of having my little brother to complain about. Everything ran smoothly. There were no hiccups and all the work got done.

But then, the rains didn't come when we expected them to. Some of the crops failed and we were worried about the harvest. Then our best cow died and then a few of the sheep. It was a worrying time. For weeks there was no rain at all. Fortunately we'd had a bumper harvest a number of years running and had plenty of grain set aside. No one on our land would go hungry and Dad was very generous to all the servants and their families. But soon the ground began to dry up almost entirely. It was hard to carry water from the river to the fields. The river soon began to get brown and muddy then patchy. And then it stopped flowing altogether.

But then, miracle of miracles, it rained! It rained so hard

that the drops bounced off the dry earth and formed huge puddles. The animals drank greedily from the troughs and we breathed a sigh of relief.

Each night after dinner it was my father's habit to go and sit on the roof. He would just sit and wait. He wouldn't come down until he was almost asleep. Some nights I sat with him, just to keep him company, although I always turned my chair towards the fields and not the road. I knew that my brother was not coming home.

One day we had a friend of ours visit – a merchant – come to buy some of our grain. He told us that the lack of rain had affected many of the crops in surrounding cities and towns. Hoards of people were hungry and had been growing desperate. The price of grain was very high. Just as we loaded up the last of the sacks onto his camels, he beckoned me over to the barn. He clearly had something to tell me.

Waiting until my father was out of earshot he said, "I have seen Joe. He is in the big city near the mountains. You know the one? I saw him in a … a sort of hotel. I was feeding the camels outside and there he was, drunk as a skunk and surrounded by laughing women with lots of flesh on show. It made my heart sad to see it. But I thought I should tell you that at least he is still alive."

I didn't know what to say. I was not surprised. But I was angry. The anger boiled up inside of me. He was wasting the money. I had always known he would, but now that I had heard he actually was, I felt sick.

I had earnt that money with years of sweat from my brow. I had watched my Mum earn that money selling cloth that she had dyed and spun herself. I had seen my Dad spend hours in the fields working out how many crops to sow, when to harvest and what price to sell them at. This was hard earnt money from our family and it was being WASTED.

I didn't want to tell my Dad. I didn't want to tell him anything, but I had to say what I knew. I couldn't hide it.

That evening as we sat on the roof, I told him I had heard news of Joe.

"Is he coming home?" he asked, suddenly excited and beaming.

"No Dad. No, I am so sorry, Reuben the merchant saw him in the city. He was drunk and he was surrounded by women, the kind of women who perhaps weren't, you know, all that holy..."

My dad was quiet.

"Thank you for telling me," he said simply.

"Let's go to bed."

He patted me on the shoulder as we parted.

I was so angry. Joe wasn't even here and he was still hurting Dad. How dare he?

Things continued as normal. I still couldn't persuade Dad inside in the evenings. Even when it was freezing cold Dad would sit under an animal skin trying to warm himself as he waited.

"What is he hoping for?" my friends asked.

"He doesn't really think your brother is actually coming home does he? I mean, it's more likely he will drink himself to death!"

Sadly I had to agree. Joe had never been wise. I wondered how long the money would last. I wondered how many women he had slept with and how many slanderous things he had said about our lovely, generous Dad. I shuddered.

It wasn't that much later in the year when it started to get really chilly at night. I thought Dad would catch cold up there on his own, so I built him a kind of fire in a metal container. It made him happy to sit there and watch the flames dance around. He stayed up there for hours. Just watching and waiting and hoping. He never seemed to think it was time to give up.

One day I had to go to market to gauge the price for some new heifers. I was gone for the whole day and didn't get back until night fall. I was exhausted when I reached our fields and needed a long drink and a rest. But as I was nearing the house, I could hear music. All the lamps were burning and the whole place was lit up. The lights spilled out from every window – just like when Mum was alive and we were having a party.

I checked myself.

As I walked towards the house I found a servant running out to fetch more wine.

"What is going on?" I asked him

"Your brother has returned," he told me "and your Dad has thrown a huge party for everyone. People have come from miles away. Your aunts and uncles are all here. Go in and see!"

Suddenly there was a stale metallic taste in my mouth. The smell of competition was in the air. Jealous bitterness rose in my throat and threatened to choke me.

"What?" I cried, not believing him. "What do you mean? How can he be home?"

"The story is that he ran out of money and ended up feeding

pigs, sir," the servant told me. "Then he realised he would be better off at home and came back."

"Typical" I thought. "He comes back because he is hungry. He comes back because he has wasted everything. He comes back stinking of pigs."

I breathed hard. I couldn't go in. I couldn't be happy. This was not how I thought it would go.

And then my Dad came out to see me.

He was crying with joy. He embraced me and held me tight.

"Your brother is home!" he said "He is back as if from the dead. He is alive and well and safe and he is here. Come and see him. He's so thin and he looks ill. But some good food and care will help him. Come with me, David, please."

"How can you take him back? How can you do this?" I said. "After all he has lost. That was our money Dad. It was our reputation. It was our family name that he dragged through that dirty pig pen."

I looked through the door to see the table laden with a feast bigger than I had ever seen.

"Did you ... did you kill the calf we were fattening up to sell? I can't believe it. All these years I've been slaving for you and never disobeyed your orders. Yet you never gave me even a young goat so I could have a little party with my friends. But when this son of yours who has squandered your property with prostitutes comes home, you kill the best calf for him! And you invite all the neighbours. That calf cost money to feed, Dad, lots of money!"

Dad looked at me earnestly.

"My son, I love you," he said. "You have been so good. You have stayed with me and worked hard. You're always with me and everything I have is yours. But we had to celebrate and be glad, because this brother of yours was dead and is alive again; he was lost and now is found."

Then my brother himself came to the door. He was wearing Dad's best robe and he had a signet ring on his hand and clean, new sandals on his feet. I winced inwardly. "He's back for five minutes and already dressed better than me," I thought. But as I looked into his face, I was shocked. He looked awful, really awful – gaunt and thin and pale and ill. All of the spark and brashness was gone. He was worried and anxious. Then he spoke.

"David, I am so sorry. I don't deserve to be your brother, or Dad's son. I have told him to treat me like a slave, but he won't listen. Talk to him! Reason with him! I don't deserve all this. It's embarrassing to be the centre of attention as if I've done something amazing, when I have failed you both, so badly!" His voice trailed off.

He looked and sounded as though he meant it. As though he meant every word. He was leaning against the doorframe. Suddenly he closed his eyes and his body slumped. I thought he was going to faint. He fell into me and I caught him and lifted him into my arms. He weighed hardly anything.

Suddenly I remembered I was the big brother. I was the wise one. I was the one that held the family together. I had to think quickly. I was about to offer to take him to the barn and lie him on some straw, but Dad interrupted my thoughts.

"David, take him to his room," said Dad urgently. "Let him sleep."

Reluctantly, I took him and lay him on his bed. I pulled the robe around him like blanket. It was the warmest robe in the whole house. Mum had made it for Dad and it still reminded me of her. I took off his sandals. They were way too big for him. Even his feet seemed skinny and old. Then I looked at the ring on his finger and my jealousy rose up once more. That ring had belonged to my Mother's father. It was a family ring – a special one.

Suddenly Dad was behind me. As if he could hear what I was thinking, he spoke.

"David, everything in this house belongs to you. Everything. Look at your own robe, look at your own ring and your own sandals. You have always had everything you've needed right here."

I turned to him and whispering angrily I spat, "But I worked for it Dad! I never left you or squandered your money or debased myself with other women like HE has. I have kept myself clean and pure. He ... he comes home filthy and ragged and you treat him the SAME as me. That's not fair."

"Love isn't fair," Dad responded. "Blessing has no favourites. You seem to have forgotten what being in this family is all about. It's not what you do that matters to me. Was Joe still my son when he left? Was he still my son in the brothel? Was he still my son in the pigsty? Of course he was. You would still be my son, even if you had done all these things too. My love for you isn't because you work hard and get me good prices at the market or because you store our grain well. It's because you're my son. Now please, come downstairs and have some food with me. You must be starving after a long day."

I smiled. I was defeated.

"Yes, Dad, I am," I said.

We went down arm in arm.

And that night as I enjoyed the best BBQ'd beef I have ever tasted and endured the wet sloppy kisses of my aunts and cousins, those words pulsed through my veins.

I was loved. I was home.

I didn't have to try any more.

* * *

Like this character, God wants us to realise how loved we are; that we have our home in Him and that we don't have to strive for His affection and approval.

How do you feel about that?

Perhaps you need to admit for the first time, or all over again, that you have worth and value. Maybe you need to reflect on the part of that story that impacted you the most.

You might want to write your reflections down. In my experience, it is helpful to record how you feel when God is challenging you. Keeping a note of it means that when you return to it you can see where and how He has been at work.

Living securely means we need to know how loved we are and understand more about who it is that loves us. The next chapter will help us identify some practical tools to help us do this every day.

6
Security Measures

[practical aids for security]

"Human nature dictates that most often we will be as insecure as we are self-absorbed. The best possible way to keep from getting sucked into the superficial narcissistic mentality that money, possessions and sensuality can satisfy and secure us is to deliberately give ourselves to something much greater."
– Beth Moore

This chapter is going to look at ways to build and maintain our security levels. God knows that we need a battle-tested security system and He has given all the resources necessary.

These include:
- Reading and believing the Bible
- Declaring the truths of the Bible
- Keeping a prayer journal
- Writing a kindness book
- Going on regular retreats
- Having a prayer triplet
- Being part of a thriving church

- Being part of a small group
- Maintaining good eating and fitness habits
- Getting enough sleep
- Practicing financial generosity and good spending
- Surrounding yourself with encouragers
- Confession and forgiveness
- Knowing who we are in Christ
- Visualisations
- Soaking in God's presence

All these things have an impact on our security.

Let's look at them briefly in turn.

TAKE YOUR MEDICINE

If ever you are ill and need medicine, there is no point in it staying in the cupboard. If you have a fever or a backache you have to take the medicine in the way it has been prescribed, until you feel better.

Many of us think we can go through life without medicating and feeding ourselves on God's word. We face all sorts of trials and pain, but God's word stays on the shelf or in the cupboard. I am always amazed that we can live like this when we have such open access to our own healing.

There must be a bad joke somewhere about Moses having a headache and God telling him to take two large tablets for it?!

But it is true. The Bible, the laws of God are like medicine for us. Psalm 119:103 says, *"How sweet are your words to my taste, sweeter than honey to my mouth!"*

The words that God has provided are good for us. They taste GOOD and do us good.

BELIEVE IT!

The following 10 verses are TRUTH to help you combat insecurity. If you are feeling low, copy these verses out and put them somewhere you can see them on a daily basis. But, take my advice here, do not merely read them in your heart, SAY them out loud. The atmosphere in our hearts and homes can change when we make declarations of truth. This is also something we are encouraged to do in Scripture. Revelation 1:3 says:

> *"Blessed is the one who reads aloud the words of this prophecy, and blessed are those who hear it and take to heart what is written in it, because the time is near."*

1. *"There is therefore now no condemnation for those who are in Christ Jesus."* (Romans 8:1)

2. *"The LORD will fulfill his purpose for me; your steadfast love, O LORD, endures forever. Do not forsake the work of your hands."* (Psalm 138:8)

3. *"...for you were bought with a price. So glorify God in your body."* (1 Corinthians 6:20)

4. *"To the praise of the glory of his grace, wherein he hath made us accepted in the beloved."* (Ephesians 1:6)

5. *"The Spirit himself bears witness with our spirit that we are children of God, and if children, then heirs – heirs of God and fellow heirs with Christ, provided we suffer with him in order that we may also be glorified with him."* (Romans 8:16-17)

6. "...being confident of this very thing, that He who has begun a good work in you will complete it until the day of Jesus Christ." (Philippians 1:6)

7. "But God, being rich in mercy, because of the great love with which he loved us ... raised us up with him and seated us with him in the heavenly places in Christ Jesus." (Ephesians 2:4 and v6)

8. "But you are a chosen race, a royal priesthood, a holy nation, a people for his own possession, that you may proclaim the excellencies of him who called you out of darkness into his marvelous light." (1 Peter 2:9)

9. "For we are his workmanship, created in Christ Jesus for good works, which God prepared beforehand, that we should walk in them." (Ephesians 2:10)

10. "I am he who blots out your transgressions for my own sake, and I will not remember your sins." (Isaiah 43:25)

Aren't those verses amazing? They tell us so much about God's heart towards us – about His unconditional love, His forgiveness and His grace. Let's not try to live as though we can handle life without those things!

DECLARE IT

As well as speaking out the truth of Scripture, we can also make some declarations based on verses from the Bible. I used to think this was a bit flaky and based on the way disingenuous TV evangelists speak, but God has opened my eyes. I only started praying like this a couple of years ago, after reading a book by Stormie Omartian, but it has completely revolutionised how I pray over myself. (Something I rarely did before). For example we can say things over ourselves like: "God is on my side. Therefore I declare today that I cannot be defeated, discouraged, depressed or disappointed." (This declaration is based on Romans 8:37, Psalm 91 and Philippians 4:13)

Can you see how crazily powerful that is to speak out?

We all know that, at times, the enemy comes to us and wants us to feel defeat, discouragement, lack, depression and disappointment. But this declaration speaks out the opposite truth. If I say this over myself first thing in the morning, I am readying myself for the day. It is part of me putting on the full armour of God (see Ephesians 6:10-18).

I now have a list of declarations above my desk permanently. Whenever I sit there, I will speak them out. I know I need to take my daily medicine.

You can write your own declarations once you have found some powerful scriptures that mean a great deal to you and are relevant to your situation. These might be simple such as:

God loves me.

He wants to speak to me.

I can hear from God.

He is faithful to me.

He is leading me.

All of these things are true and you will find multiple Bible verses telling you so. Or your declarations can be longer and incorporate truth from a number of verses such as:

My prayers are powerful and effective (2 Corinthians 5:21, James 5:16b).

God will use them and other blessings to richly supply all my needs (Philippians 4:19).

I walk in ever increasing health (Isaiah 53:3-5, Psalm 103:1-3).

I live under supernatural protection (Psalm 91).

I will prosper in all my relationships (Luke 2:52).

Through Jesus I am worthy to receive all of God's blessings (Galatians 3:1-5).

Can you see what this means?

It means you are starting to tell yourself what God has already told you!

If you gather and write your own verses up, they will mean much more to you than just finding someone else's list and using that, so I am deliberately not giving you mine! I want you to search for your own treasure.

I am privileged to have the most wonderful mentor at the moment. One of the things she told me at our first meeting is that second-hand Bible knowledge i.e. learning from other people, is all well and good, but actually it can be a bit like baby food. It's all mushed up and often looks wildly unappetizing. You are unsure where it has come from and exactly what it is you are eating. It could be spinach or broccoli, carrot or sweet potato! When we go to the word of God ourselves, what we are eating is fresh and clean. It is not regurgitated, left over, or a revelation someone else has had. So let me encourage you to get into the Bible for yourself. By all means use commentaries, Bible reading notes, and anything you need to as an aid – but do not do this BEFORE having read it yourself.

Declaring truth over yourself and reading the Bible in this way can make you stronger, braver and wiser. It is not wishful thinking, mindfulness or simply practicing being positive. It is allowing your spirit to get in line with things God has already said about you and about Himself. It is reminding yourself of the strength of God and the purposes He has for you. I can't recommend it enough.

KEEPING A JOURNAL

I am a writer so I am bound to enjoy and need to write things down. But I do think it is a useful tool for anyone to employ. I have kept a prayer journal since I was about 9. I find it so helpful to be able to look at the promises God has made me, as well as the prayers He has answered. In this last year, I made a column of prayer requests that I was going to pray specifically each week. God answered every single one! He did everything I needed – not always in the way that I thought, but He did answer each prayer. I can't tell you how joyful I was as I ticked off each prayer need. This has given me the faith to start a whole new column!

Think about this for a minute. If God answered every single prayer you prayed last week would you be elated or disappointed you didn't pray for more?

I am learning that God wants us to be specific and targeted in our praying. He wants us to pray the prayers on His heart. So taking time to listen before we spout is always a great idea!

If you don't currently have a prayer journal, please buy a notebook to use. It is such a useful tool for your growth and inner security. It can also be helpful when you are praying with others. One of the girls I mentor brings her journal to our sessions. She will sometimes read passages from it or show me things God has said, so that I can fully understand her and can pray with her better.

A KINDNESS BOOK

I am a huge fan of Joyce Meyer. I love so much about her ministry and have been massively inspired by many of her books I have read. One of the things she encouraged me to do was to start a book of things that God does for me – things that nobody else would notice. I call it my "Kindness Book".

In it, I keep a note of all the secret ways in which God blesses me. Some are small and some are giant. They are not answers to prayer, because I haven't prayed for them, they are blessings and signposts of His love for me.

Since I have kept my kindness book (which has been a fairly recent addition to my world) I have begun to notice how often God chooses to love me and bless me. Sometimes these things could be missed. Writing them down reminds me how good He is to me on a daily basis and how much I have to thank Him for.

I thought you might like to see some of my entries. You may think these are tiny things, but to me they show me He is at work:

"Thank you for putting my friend in the shop I was in today, at just the right time, to guide me to a cheap pair of shoes I needed for a wedding outfit."

"Thank you for helping me bake a batch of cookies and get 30 out of the mixture, which was just how many I needed."

These aren't answers to long, drawn-out prayers. They are

just small ways in which I see God at work in my day, in the mundane, everyday things.

At the front of my kindness book I have written:

"This is the book to record everything God does for me that no one else would notice – the secret ways in which He loves me. Some of them are small but they are all significant parts of my story."

Perhaps you could start a Kindness Book too?

GOING ON REGULAR RETREATS

I have learnt in the last few years that I need to spend some focused time every few months alone with God. This means that I need to prioritise that time and make it happen. It won't just suddenly jump into my diary! I have to pray about it and ask God to help me. My husband is brilliant at caring for the kids when I am away. I have sometimes felt guilty about going, but I am learning that everyone benefits from a change. The children and Jon react very well to a refreshed and rejuvenated me!

The benefits of a retreat are incredible. Taking time out to sit with God without any other distractions helps you stay focused on what He is calling you to do. It is a precious time to listen and read and think. Often I come away from such a time more creative, more determined and more at peace. I am certainly more able to take on what God has next for me. Occasionally, I will be able to tackle something I have put off or speak to someone about a difficult issue with more discernment.

If you have never been away for a night or two alone to spend time with God, let me recommend it to you.

You don't need to stay in a posh hotel or even a designated retreat house. You might be able to stay for a night with family or friends and use their house whilst they are at work. Make sure you are alone, otherwise it won't feel restful. Many of my friends in Manchester have provided me with their houses for a day or two. One of the most precious retreats I had this year was just staying at my brother's house in Liverpool. God spoke to me so deeply there. So a retreat needn't be costly.

There are plenty of places you can go. Your local area will have a retreat house for clergy or youth workers. A quick search on the Internet should show you your options. If not, ask a local church leader where they would recommend.

I think everyone needs to spend focused time like this with God, whatever job they do and whatever their normal world looks like. You might argue with me on this one, but try it. You might change your mind.

People have often asked me what I take on retreat with me. It will vary depending on what you need and who you are, but here is what I take, to help me both relax and pray:

A candle and matches.

My Bible and notebook and a few pens.

Some Christian books I haven't read yet.

Some simple food (if cooking for myself).

A treat, such as a magazine or posh coffee.

Some clay or crayons and paper – if you are a creative person.

Some music and headphones.

Walking boots (often going for a long walk is part of my praying).

Warm, comforting clothes.

A hot water bottle (some places I have stayed in are chilly).

My prayer journal.

My Kindness Book.

On some retreats I have rested, on others I have written or been creative. It has been just what I have needed at that time. I have learnt not to go with a huge shopping list of things to ask God about. I try to let Him set the agenda for the time. And He always has.

HAVING A PRAYER TRIPLET

I have always enjoyed praying with others. When I was a little girl my Grandma and Grandpa used to take me to early morning prayer meetings and I loved sitting with other sweet people petitioning the Lord. This gave me an appetite for prayer. I have always wanted to pray with people ever since.

I am currently part of a prayer triplet. We love hanging out together to pray. I honestly know that I would not be who I am without these two voices in my life and I know they would say the same. They have been there for me when I have been challenged and stretched by life. They have continued to love me and remind me what I carry. If I have doubted God's promises they have helped me recall them and I have had the opportunity and privilege to do that for them too.

I don't think it is any coincidence that the words Prayer Triplet and Personal Training share the same initials. PTs of both kinds make us stronger!

What are the benefits of my PT?

Accountability – my PT help me stay on track.

Empathy – my PT feel for me and help me through problems.

Prayer support – my PT commit to praying with me and

for me.

Prophetic – my PT are used by God to bring me verses, words of encouragement, dreams and pictures. They also help interpret ones God gives to me.

Understanding – my PT help me to work out what God is doing and saying in my life.

Protection – my PT help me stay protected and strong against the enemy.

Being part of such a prayer group is vital for my spiritual growth.

You may simply have a prayer partner and share everything with that one person. That is great too, although I have always found that there is something precious about the dynamic of three people to pray with and for.

If you don't currently pray with anyone, let me ask you to think and pray about doing it. Often people say they are too busy to organise it. But with our world of Skype and Facetime, it's easy to chat, even when you can't actually meet. And Facetime is better than no time!

BEING PART OF A THRIVING CHURCH

I have been a member of some very diverse churches in my life. I grew up as a vicar's daughter so spent the early years of my life within an Anglican setting. As a student I went to a URC church. As I grew older and got married I broadened my horizons further by embracing my husband's denomination, which was Baptist. We went to two Baptist churches, one large one and a few years later, one much smaller family one. When we moved to Manchester we joined a thriving movement called Ivy. I loved the history of this church and everything it stood for. I still do. I can honestly say that I hate missing a Sunday if I am away because I love my church family so much.

I love how God uses me there and how He uses others to bless me. On any given day I will receive a text message from someone asking for urgent prayer, or a surprise present from another person telling me they love and value me. It is a constantly growing group of wonderful people.

In the last few years God has really blessed us as a family through Ivy's ministry. I don't know what would have happened to us if we had not been there. But we certainly would not have been as brave. We would not have stepped out in faith as much as we have. We would not have been as stretched or as multiplied.

Our church calls us to fellowship with those who are different to us. It challenges us to go deeper with God. It opens our minds to great teaching and allows us to access and praise God in wonderful worship. It gives us opportunities to stretch our faith by giving generously in all seasons and it has given us the funniest most creative and inspiring group of friends we have ever had. Our leaders are people I would go under a bus for and I trust them with my life, my spiritual health, the growth of my kids and our finances.

If you aren't part of a church you are missing something vital, but also a whole group of people are missing out on you! You are meant to be part of a Christian community – to do life with others and to share in their world. There is nothing like it.

You might ask how you find a good church. Have a look online for one near to you. Many churches now have a website and you can access talks from their leaders online. This is a great way to learn what the church is like. But the best way is to check it out for yourself. I believe that you know the strength of a church not by how many people come, but by what the members do as a result of coming. So try and ask people questions about how church impacts their week.

BEING PART OF A SMALL GROUP

For years Jon and I have run a small group. However busy I am I always try to model this as a priority in my diary and in my life. It is sometimes inconvenient to host a bunch of hungry people when you are tired and life is overwhelming, but nothing keeps you more grounded.

Sharing on a more intimate level with a smaller group of people helps us stay humble. It gives us ideas and creative practical solutions to problems we are facing. It gives us the strength to continue when life gets tough. It gives us instant access to the prayers and ideas of others. It allows us to make space in the week to work out our faith. It gives us time to make friends with those we don't yet know. It helps us discuss and understand the Bible better.

Maybe you aren't in a position to lead a group and you could go to one, but choose not to. I find this alarming. No one is so important or busy that they can't, in some way, be part of a small group of believers.

MAINTAINING GOOD EATING AND FITNESS HABITS

You may wonder what healthy eating and fitness has to do with feeling secure. Plenty. If you stuff your body with things that aren't good for you, you will feel mentally and physically weak and this can quickly lead to feelings of insecurity. Being overweight, or underweight, feeling achy and lacking exercise can all be problematic. I know that my diet and my fitness is so linked to my emotional health. If I have eaten well, treated my body well, then my mind feels more in line with the truths and promises of God. But if I have become too intimate with a packet of donuts, life can feel a bit harder!

There is nothing wrong with eating. In fact God loves us to eat well and enjoy our food. The Bible says that this is one of His presents to us.

Ecclesiastes 3:12-13 (ESV) says,

"I perceived that there is nothing better for them than to be joyful and to do good as long as they live; also that everyone should eat and drink and take pleasure in all his toil – this is God's gift to man."

But many of us self-medicate with food or drink. We over-indulge when we are tired or feeling low. We comfort with calories.

God wants us to avoid gluttony, drunkenness or abusing our bodies in any way. He knows that this leads to feelings of self-deprecation and dissatisfaction.

If you have a sedentary job make sure you get some activity in the day by walking to work or doing stretching or exercises at your desk. I keep small weights nearby when I am writing to help me to remember to use them and get the blood flowing. A quick stretch will revitalise your body and help you work more efficiently.

GETTING ENOUGH SLEEP

One of the ways to better emotional health is making sure

we get enough shut-eye. Stress and anxiety often go hand in hand with insomnia. In turn, lack of sleep can mean we are less productive, less fruitful and less at peace. The Bible speaks clearly of sleep as being important for our well-being.

Psalm 127:2 (ESV) says, *"It is in vain that you rise up early and go late to rest, eating the bread of anxious toil; for he gives to his beloved sleep."*

Proverbs 3:24 (ESV) declares, *"If you lie down, you will not be afraid; when you lie down, your sleep will be sweet."*

Only God can give us the kind of rest we need, especially in a busy or stressful season. If you are struggling with sleep, that may be why you are battling in other areas of your life.

There are many practical ways to help yourself rest and switch off after a busy day. I recommend you adopting some simple things like never working in your bedroom, leaving your phone in another room, having at least an hour to wind down after doing any work, having a warm bath or reading.

PRACTICING FINANCIAL GENEROSITY AND GOOD SPENDING

Sometimes it is tempting to misuse our money. I know what it is to want something or envy someone else having it. But I firmly believe that God provides for me whether I live in plenty or lack.

Jon and I have sometimes lived in seasons of lack and sometimes seasons of plenty. Each time we have tried to first give away what we feel God is asking us to, then wait for Him to stretch the rest. I can honestly say that living like this has given us more financial security than any bank ever could. God simply turns up with money and resources when we need Him to. Of course, along the way He has taught us more about good stewardship and how to handle what He gives us, but He is always generous, loving and kind to us financially.

I recently asked my friends who live with no fixed income, relying on God for all their needs, to tell me what they had learnt from doing that.

One of my friends wrote this:

"God is no less lovely in your perceived lack than in the times you feel you're in abundance. He truly is all you need, the only one to never let you down and the ultimate provider."

I love that understanding. She also said,

"Comparison, discontentment and despondency can quickly claim thought space. I have never been in a place where I have wanted for anything I needed, but I have often lacked things I wanted. It all comes back to His word, His will and His heart ... and knowing that HE IS GOOD. No ands, ifs or buts. He is just good. FACT. Good to you and good for you. So He won't let you down."

Another pal said this:

"Looking back over times we've lived by faith, God has been faithful, always. He has often challenged our 'wants versus needs' and often when we've laid down luxury He has been so kind and provided those things in other ways. We were terrible at really, properly budgeting and I think it was because money came in so unpredictably and sporadically. So we were bad at saving properly for the dry months by over-spending because we had money in the 'harvest'. We now use the 'good budget' app, which means our everyday spending is logged and we have to look at what we've wasted money on: too many coffees or just general stuff we don't actually need. It makes you have a good hard, honest look at spending so would recommend that."

So, top tips:

TRUST ALWAYS

1. Give to God of personal and business incomes separately.
2. Be generous.
3. Save more than you think you should in the harvest.
4. Know what you're spending, down to the last pint of milk.
5. Budget realistically and don't go over it.

Many people lose sleep and emotional well-being because of money worries. Lack of finances can be a huge source of anxiety for us. But God understands all we need and He is a constant provider.

Matthew 6:31-33 (ESV) says:

"Therefore do not be anxious, saying, 'What shall we eat?' or 'What shall we drink?' or 'What shall we wear?' For the Gentiles seek after all these things, and your heavenly Father knows that you need them all. But seek first the kingdom of God and his righteousness, and all these things will be added to you."

If you are anxious right now about your financial situation, give it to God. Pray that He would show Himself strong and give you a way through your situation. If your problems are ongoing and serious, may I encourage you to seek advice from *Christians Against Poverty* (CAP). They have been used by God so many times to help people get out of debt and get themselves back on track with their bills and spending.

SURROUNDING YOURSELF WITH ENCOURAGERS

It is sometimes hard to be positive and have a secure mindset, especially when those around us are being negative. I have had to learn that it is fine to be close friends with people who struggle with being positive, but they should NOT be your only friends. I deliberately choose to surround myself with people who inspire and encourage me to grow and stretch my faith.

My best friends are those who speak words of life and hope into my life. When I err, they are also kind enough to challenge and confront me, because they have my express permission to do so. But they are not nay-sayers or negative mud slingers.

Think about who you allow into your inner circle and examine the most common feelings you have after being with them. Do they build you up or do they make you feel small and insecure?

1 Thessalonians 5:11 says,

"Therefore encourage one another and build one another up.."

Do you do this for your friends? Do they do it for you?

Maybe you need to examine who you are surrounded by.

CONFESSION AND FORGIVENESS

I was abused as a child and as a young person. Having this kind of background has taught me a lot about the essential nature of both confession and forgiveness in my life. I have learnt the power of confession, of telling God where I have fallen short. I believe His word when He says that if we confess our sins, He will be faithful and just and forgive us (see 1 John 1:9). I stand on that promise every time I feel I have let Him down.

I have also learnt to practice forgiveness. This is not letting the person who has hurt you "off the hook", it is deciding to let YOURSELF off carrying that hurt around with you. No one needs to bear the weight of unforgiveness. It is heavy and ugly. It bears down on you and causes you to have all sorts of emotional hang-ups and issues.

There are many ways you can practically help yourself let go of bitterness and seek to forgive those who have hurt you. One way, if you can't speak to the person in question, is to write them a letter. It doesn't ever have to be sent. It is the process that will bless you, not necessarily the outcome.

You could also imagine having a whole conversation with them. I find it useful to imagine a person who has hurt me sitting in the same room as me. I imagine making them a drink. I imagine not wanting to sneak something nasty into it! I imagine making them something special to eat and I imagine blessing them with my words and forgiving them in my heart. This is such a powerful visualisation and has helped me many times to get over an old hurt.

I think my all time favourite verse in the whole of the Bible is Isaiah 61:4 which says:

"They will rebuild the ancient ruins
and restore the places long devastated;
they will renew the ruined cities
that have been devastated for generations."

In some translations this first verse talks about being a "repairer of the breach". For many people there is a divide they can't get across. They can't forgive you for hurting them.

Or perhaps they can't forgive themselves. So let them be. You do your part and forgive them anyway. It will set you free.

We all have an in-built longing for approval and acceptance, but sometimes this will not come from someone who has hurt us. God knows this. We need to let that emotion go and allow Him to carry it for us. I don't want to continue to strive for that in an unhealthy way and I don't want you to, either.

KNOWING YOUR IDENTITY IN CHRIST

Who am I? Is a question we all ask ourselves from time to time. Being secure means understanding who we are in relation to how God sees us. There are some amazing scriptures that tell us who we are in Christ. Here are some:

"But you are a chosen race, a royal priesthood, a holy nation, a people for his own possession, that you may proclaim the excellencies of him who called you out of darkness into his marvellous light." (1 Peter 2:9)

"No longer do I call you servants, for the servant does not know what his master is doing; but I have called you friends, for all that I have heard from my Father I have made known to you." (John 15:15)

"But to all who did receive him, who believed in his name, he gave the right to become children of God." (John 1:12)

"There is therefore now no condemnation for those who are in Christ Jesus." (Romans 8:1)

"For we are God's masterpiece, created to do good works which God prepared in advance for us to do." (Ephesians 2:10)

2 Corinthians 5:17 says, *"Therefore, if anyone is in Christ, the new creation has come: the old has gone, the new is here!"*

When we become a follower of Jesus, we change on the inside. We are no longer just sinners. We are totally new people. But we forget easily who we are now. We need to remind ourselves daily.

VISUALISATIONS

A few years ago one of my best friends told me that she visualised Jesus when she was struggling with something. She asked Him to speak to her and started to hear Him talk to her in a different way. Since then I have found this practice incredibly helpful – both in praying for myself and for others too. Daniel 7:13-14 describes how Daniel saw Jesus like this too:

"I kept looking in the night visions, and behold, with the clouds of heaven One like a Son of Man was coming, and He came up to the Ancient of Days and was presented before Him. 'And to Him was given dominion, Glory and a kingdom, that all the peoples, nations and men of every language might serve Him. His dominion is an everlasting dominion which will not pass away; and His kingdom is one which will not be destroyed."

Often I will imagine Jesus sitting with me somewhere very beautiful. We will talk and I will see how He starts to change how I am feeling. Notice that the verses in Daniel speak of Jesus having total "dominion". This means power, command, control, supremacy and direction. When we pray and ask Jesus to help us He will take over and relieve us of our burdens. This is so comforting and helps us feel loved and secure again.

A.W. Tozer puts this beautifully. He says,

"God is so vastly wonderful, so utterly and completely delightful that He can, without anything other than Himself, meet and overflow the deepest demands of our total nature, mysterious and deep as that nature is."

SOAKING IN GOD'S PRESENCE

I love spending time listening to worship music and relaxing. I often do this lying down, deliberately resting and allowing myself time off and time out. I have found this to be one of the main ways that the Holy Spirit comforts and restores me. It often gives me a fresh perspective. Even familiar words to songs are imbued with deeper meaning and seem more relevant in these times.

You can do this by yourself or with a small group of others. In the last couple of years I have sometimes gathered a few other girls to pray with me in this way. They have been precious times of incredible prophetic significance for us all.

The Bit At The End

It was 6.00am. Suddenly awakened from a vivid dream I lay alert, recalling the minute details. I looked at my husband, still fast asleep and pondered how I was going to reach for my notebook and find a pen without waking him. The apartment where we were staying was filled with fresh light and although early, the air was already hot. It promised to be another scorching day in Minorca.

As I gently sat upright to avoid the worst of the squeaky sofa-bed noises, I had a sense that I was about to spill out onto the page more than just the contents of my dream.

I had dreamt very clearly of my friend Anthony, our pastor here in Manchester, earnestly telling me to finish my book. I had laughed at him and told him I already had, thinking he meant my last one. But he was insistent. "Not the one about grief," he had said, slowly and deliberately. "The next one."

I saw his face. He was sure. He was bold. He was nodding.

I then dreamt, or at least became aware of, a brief but clear outline for the book that you have just read. Complete with its simple but profound title.

As I woke up fully I could remember the 6 chapters and what each of them said – not every word, of course, but the spirit of each one. It felt like such a gift! I scribbled as fast as I could with my daughter's blue wax crayon – the only writing implement I could find. The words grew on the page and the idea progressed in my mind. The more I wrote, the more came to me. Without properly engaging my brain once there, before me, was the skeleton of a new being – a new piece of writing – a whole book. It was entirely effortless and something I can take zero credit for.

The most significant part of this dream for me is the space where nothing is written. It is the gap between the word "In" and the word "Security" on the front cover. Time and time again in recent years, God has shown me that this *gap* is vital for my well-being and my spiritual health. The further away those two words sit in our lives, the better off our children, our families and our friends will be. The larger that gap is, the more capacity for greatness we will display.

You see, to live with INSECURITY (no gap) is to be miserable; to be constantly dogged by comparison, berating ourselves and losing out on God's best for us. But to live IN SECURITY (with a big joyful gap) is the living breathing opposite. It is to live and love and laugh as He intended.

I am learning to long for that and to live that way.

I trust that reading this book will help you to do the same. I pray that my words have been useful to you and that you have made time to examine your heart as you have journeyed with me. That's the point of any book worth its salt, after all.

I will leave you with a beautiful quote from A. A. Milne which says, rather eloquently:

"What day is it?"

"It's today," squeaked Piglet.

"My favourite day," said Pooh."

Make today your favourite day by allowing God to widen the gap for you; to prise those words apart and be your security. Do not put off forgiving someone, leaving the past behind or changing the way you talk about yourself. Life is too short! Join me in the adventure of living IN SECURITY, today and always.

With love,

Ems.

P.S. If you have enjoyed my writing, there is an abundant supply at *http://emshancock.com/blog.php*

About the Author

Ems Hancock is a writer, speaker and singer based in Manchester. Her desire is to help others be the person God intended and live in healing and wholeness. She is the author of *Good Grief – Living Through Loss* and co-author (with Ian Henderson) of *Sorted – The Distinctive Guide to Life's Big Issues.* In 2010 she released her first album of original songs, *Coming Home*.

Ems is married to Jon, a Bafta award winning TV producer who has recently launched his own production company. They have three sons and a daughter.

73065342R00077

Made in the USA
Middletown, DE
10 May 2018